Not Worth Saving

How a Severely Handicapped Boy Transformed Lives

Ann L. Joyner

Praise for *Not Worth Saving*

Not Worth Saving reminds us as physicians that we are often overly pragmatic about the possibilities of cure or even improvement in patients given a set of medical facts: lab tests, X-rays, medical literature. We sometimes fail to account for the healing power of a loving family, supportive community, and strong faith. Healing is not always about perfect health.

The Joyners' story about their precious son Matthew reminds us that we often underestimate the will to live and the tremendous influence one special life can have in changing our everyday world, our families, neighborhoods, schools, and churches. We must remember to celebrate every life and to respect and nurture each individual. Our patients, children, family members, and friends with special needs have an abundance of remarkable gifts to share with all of us.

Matthew shared his joy with our whole church community and, through the efforts of his parents and many others, continues to make a difference in numerous lives. One life, blessing so many. The face of God was reflected in Matthew's bright eyes and smile, and continues to be reflected in all our children and adults with special needs. We can see God if we take the time to live life with them.

Betse M. Gage, MD
William M. Chase, MD
Parents of a child with special needs
Leawood, KS

Meeting Ann Joyner at the Leadership Institute, and witnessing the abundant love and tender care offered to special needs families through Matthew's Ministry at Church of the Resurrection in Kansas City, influenced and inspired us to launch Donovan's Door, a now thriving special needs ministry for children and families at Los Altos United Methodist Church in California. When she spoke to our congregation on Mother's Day, her testimony opened our hearts and moved many to serve as volunteers in Donovan's Door. The depth and breadth of Ann's faith and her perseverance in the face of adversity is a testament to God's grace working through her actions and her words, and remind us all again that every single child is a beloved child of God.

Lisa Conway, children's ministries director
Los Altos United Methodist Church
Los Altos, CA

God tends to use foolishness to shame the wise and weakness to thwart the strong. Just when the smartest among us declared that Matthew Joyner's life was a life not worth saving, God made those words sound foolish and used that life to bless thousands of lives in his short span of 21 years. Ann Joyner has shared the compelling story of Matthew, the child whom she, Jerry, and big brother, Drew, shared with the world in so many ways. Your heart will be blessed and your spirit soar as you read the timeless stories of how God has worked through the love of the church, of friends, and the devotion of two parents and a big brother who set out on a journey in 1984 to prove to the world that this was more than a life worth saving. This was Matthew—a gift of God!

Dr. Jeff Smith, senior pastor
Wellspring United Methodist Church
Georgetown, TX

God's love has the ability to make sense out of nonsensical things. It connects the disconnected. It has the ability to endure great distances in order to draw people together from all over to experience the life that really is life. Matthew's story embodies the awesome power of God's amazing love as demonstrated through the life of a child, his family, and a community of faith all seeking to change the world. It is definitely a story worth saving.

Scott Chrostek, pastor
United Methodist Church of the Resurrection Downtown
Kansas City, MO

Expressing the powerfully positive and long-lasting impact that an individual with special needs can have on others is no easy task. Ann Joyner's Not Worth Saving is able to capture and convey the many ways in which her son Matthew taught—and still teaches, through his legacy—life's most valuable lessons.

Ann openly shares the constant challenges that come with parenting a child with special needs. These parents and caregivers must see their children as individuals and write their own guidebooks centered on their own definitions of normal. Ann mentions in the book that it didn't take her long as a new mom before she threw away the parenting book identifying all of a child's developmental milestones. As a mother of a young child with autism, I can relate.

Ann and her husband, Jerry, reveal that—although the challenges vary in size and number when parenting a child with special needs—love, faith, humor, hope, and determination can serve as your constant and saving grace through anything. Throughout their story, the Joyners emphasize the importance of embracing the gifts of the present and pushing forward the best you know how. Ann exemplifies this in her ability to organize and lead Matthew's villages. Ann established these villages of supporters in whichever state they resided so that Matthew and the family were never alone in their journeys. Ultimately, she knew that those around Matthew needed him just as much as Matthew needed them.

Lindsay Applebaugh, special education teacher
Mother of a child with special needs
Denver, CO

Dedicated to
Jerry, my other rock
and
Drew, Matthew's hero

Contents

FOREWORD

I first met Ann Joyner on a snowy Monday more than twenty years ago. She and Jerry had visited our church, then meeting in an elementary school gym, the day before. I stopped by to deliver a coffee mug as a sign of our welcome, and to invite them to worship with us again.

Little did I know how much that visit would affect my life, much less the church where I serve. As I stood at the door, coffee mug in hand, Ann invited me into her home and introduced me to her nine-year-old son, Matthew, who sat in a glider chair, rocking back and forth. Matthew was a beautiful child but also clearly a child with disabilities. Ann said, "We enjoyed visiting your church, but Mattie, our youngest child, has special needs that would be difficult for a smaller congregation to meet."

In that moment I knew our three-year-old congregation of two hundred people would do whatever it took to be a church family to Ann, Matthew, Jerry, and Drew. I asked her to get me a list of what he needed, and promised to start a ministry for him within two weeks. That was the beginning of my relationship with the Joyners, and the beginning of a profound and wonderful journey our congregation would have with them, and in ministry to persons with special needs.

In the years since that day, the congregation and I came to love Matthew and his family. When Matthew passed several years ago, I had the privilege of celebrating his life, and as we did, we recognized that the one whom doctors said would be a "life not worth saving" had touched more than twenty thousand people in our congregation, tens of thousands of others in the Kansas City area, and still thousands more across the United States.

Matthew's story is closely intertwined with the stories of Ann, Jerry, and Drew. Ann is a dynamo. She's outgoing, friendly, determined, and the kind of person who makes things happen. Jerry is compassionate, humble, and kind; a guy who would do whatever it takes to help another. Their oldest son, Drew, is in many ways the best of both of his parents. What is clear to me is that Matthew played a key part in shaping the very best parts of each of their lives. I don't know whom they would have been had he not been born. I feel confident Matthew changed their lives for the better.

This is the impact special needs people can have on those around them. They often draw out from us compassion, kindness, humility, gentleness, and patience. We're not meant to romanticize the challenges they and their families face. But we are meant to see the profound impact persons with special needs often have on the world.

Adam Hamilton, senior pastor
United Methodist Church of the Resurrection
Leawood, KS

(For more information about Matthew's Ministry at the Church of the Resurrection, please visit our website at *www.cor.org*.)

INTRODUCTION

Imagine being told the child developing inside you is a life that's "not worth saving." I am the woman who was told that. My son Matthew was that child. This is our story.

I would describe my life before Matthew as ordinary. Growing up, I dreamed of getting married, having a couple of kids, and living in the suburbs—just like my mom. After attending secretarial college, I went to work, where I met Jerry. Shortly thereafter, we married, and our first son, Drew, was born to us four years later.

From my perspective, my life had been predictable. And perfect. In fact, it had been very predictable. And very perfect—until the day our second son, Matthew, came along. He turned my world, and the world of everyone around him, upside down.

Faced with raising a child I had been told was not worth saving, the expected became the unexpected. The perfect was suddenly imperfect. The possibilities morphed into impossibilities.

Or, could it be the other way around?

In Hebrew, Matthew means *gift from God*. All good gifts are meant to share. It is with a humble and grateful heart that I am able to share our Matthew—our gift—with you.

Ours is a story written for people looking for a message of hope. My wish is for it to motivate you to become victorious, finding joy and light to replace feelings of despair and darkness, in all circumstances.

Part One

God as Your Ally

1 Whom Do You Turn To?

With God all things are possible.
-Matthew 19:26

First Light

There was never any doubt when I was pregnant with my first child, Drew, that I experienced the normal stages of pregnancy. First, incredible waves of morning sickness hit me when I least expected, followed by several weeks of being so tired I felt like a bear that had gone into hibernation. I blamed my lack of energy on the sixty-nine days of temperatures over one hundred degrees that summer in Arlington, Texas. All I wanted to do was stand in a pool or sit under a fan to keep cool. Then the weight started piling on, spreading over every inch of my 5'8" frame. I was huge. My total weight gain was sixty pounds; the day I gave birth to Drew, I weighed more than my dear husband, Jerry. (Why do people consider this normal?)

Not all parts of being pregnant with Drew were awful or uncomfortable. I'll never forget that first miraculous kick I felt. It was more like a tiny butterfly flapping its wings. This special movement occurred sometime during my fifth month. The butterfly turned into a hummingbird for the duration of the pregnancy. Constant movement in my belly happily reminded me each minute that I carried a baby inside me.

During labor, it felt as though there were a thousand knives being inserted, twisted, and turned over a fourteen-hour period. Then, finally, another cry suddenly drowned out my own; it was strong, and accompanied by the flailing arms and legs of my first baby, a healthy boy.

Andrew Allen Joyner, whom we call Drew, came into this world on October 29, 1980, after what was considered a normal delivery. Once again, the reference to labor as "normal" is a bit bewildering. What could possibly be normal about what my body had gone through?

Two and a half years passed before I became pregnant with my second child. Pregnancy with Matthew was an entirely different feeling and experience. From the beginning, it never felt quite right. For starters, the only reason I suspected I might be pregnant was that I missed a period. A visit to the doctor confirmed my suspicion. Our family of three was excited.

Early in the pregnancy, over the Fourth of July holiday, we headed to Jerry's brother's house in Houston. We stopped in the hill country of Texas along the way, choosing to spend one night at a small hotel. At two and a half years of age, Drew felt the outdoor pool beckoning.

Jerry and Drew quickly changed into their swimsuits, leaving me behind to organize our tiny hotel room and change into my swimsuit. When I did, fear consumed me. There was blood in my underwear. Suddenly, I could barely breathe. I felt like I was being strangled.

After leaving many messages on a recording at my obstetrician's office back in Arlington, I finally received a response to my desperate calls. The nurse assured me that spotting early in pregnancy was quite common. However, if really heavy bleeding developed, that would be a sign I was probably miscarrying. If that happened, I was to go to the nearest hospital.

For the next two days, I held my breath and prayed. The spotting subsided. Weeks later, I was still anxious about the possibility of miscarrying. When I talked about my fear with my doctor or friends, I was told that a miscarriage was nature's way of taking care of a defective fetus.

I never spotted again throughout the pregnancy, nor did I have morning sickness, unusual tiredness, or weight gain. But I also never had that wonderful glow that usually comes with pregnancy. And, worst of all, I never felt the butterfly. My baby was not moving.

I started telling the doctors, nurses, and anyone who would listen, "It's not right. Something is wrong with my baby."

The typical response was, "All pregnancies are different, and you should not be comparing this to your first one."

When I was six and a half months pregnant and still insisting there was something wrong, my OB/GYN agreed to order a sonogram just to pacify me. I felt like I had won a huge battle because, in 1983, sonograms were rarely performed.

Jerry was not overly concerned at this point, choosing to accept the reasoning that, as the doctor had suggested, all pregnancies were different. I went for the sonogram appointment on my own, just as I had for all my previous doctor visits.

When I arrived for the appointment, my apprehension was put to rest by the technician who called me from the waiting room. Her broad smile and carefree attitude washed away most of my tension. "Let's take a look at your little one, okay?" I prayed silently for the good news that my baby was fine.

As the technician moved the sonogram wand over my tiny belly, her behavior changed. I could tell from her eyes that she didn't like what she saw on the small TV screen in front of her. She continued to capture every image possible over a period of time that felt like eternity. In reality, it only took about half an hour.

All I can remember her saying was, "Well, I can tell it's a boy, and he's rather small for your stage of pregnancy." She was very businesslike at this point and stated, without a smile, "Your doctor will be in touch." Left alone in the room to gather my belongings, fear wrapped its ugly arms around me.

I went home to wait for the call from the doctor. He had gone to the hospital that morning to deliver a baby, and the technician hadn't been sure when he would be able to view all the films. The waiting and praying began.

When the doctor finally called me at home, he apologetically acknowledged, "Perhaps your concerns were valid. It appears there are some problems with your baby boy, and I would like you to go to Dallas for further testing."

I hoped the problems he referred to would be relatively small ones. After all, if this baby boy I was carrying was horribly defective, why had I not miscarried this past summer in the hill country of Texas during our vacation?

From Light to Darkness

A few days later, Jerry and I headed to Dallas for a repeat sonogram. The results were disconcerting. It appeared a valve connecting our baby's bladder to his ureter was not functioning correctly, resulting in urine backing up into his kidneys.

Not to worry. The doctors explained there was a relatively new and easy-to-do intrauterine procedure being performed in San Francisco. Our little guy could be fixed. The Dallas team of doctors would forward all their findings to the team in San Francisco for a second opinion and to nail down the scheduling of our trip. We went home, once again waiting for a phone call, praying.

The next call came, three days later, from the coordinator of the Dallas group. It had been brought to their attention by the surgeons in San Francisco that there was more wrong with our little guy than just a simple, malfunctioning valve. They had pored over the pictures and images that had been forwarded to them. Certain images on the films led them to believe our child had spina bifida. If that were the case, they would not operate on the defective valve. Further testing was suggested.

An amniocentesis was performed in Dallas the following

week. This is a risky procedure involving the removal of a sample of amniotic fluid to test for any genetic disorders. Because I was in the third trimester of my pregnancy at this stage, they explained that there was an elevated chance of miscarriage. What were our choices? We had to find out if there was anything wrong besides the valve, and how we could fix it.

I lay on the exam table, looking at our baby's outline on the sonogram screen. The doctor carefully studied where to insert the large needle in my belly so he could extract the amniotic fluid. If the needle were not inserted in just the right spot, our baby could die.

Matthew started to move. *Why now?* I thought, softly praying he would be still. The reason we were there in the first place was that I *hadn't* felt him move. His timing was not good. *Is it a sign? A sign for what?* I argued to myself.

Matthew became still, the needle was carefully inserted, and the fluid needed for the test was withdrawn. Jerry and I headed back to the suburbs to wait. I experienced cramping but no miscarriage. This seven-month-old fetus hung on for dear life.

With another week behind us, the call finally came, and the results of the amniocentesis were in. Jerry and I drove in silence to Parkland Hospital in Dallas for the appointment. Typical December weather prevailed; it was cold, gray, and rainy. After passing through the same place through which President Kennedy passed on the day of his death, Jerry and I made our way to the elevators just beyond the emergency room entrance. The slow ride in the elevator to the floor that housed the medical offices felt like eternity.

The doors of the elevator opened, and we were ushered into the conference room, which held several doctors and specialists in genetics. *Why are there so many people invited to hear the results of a test for our unborn child?*

That cold and gray day suddenly became worse. As the results of the amniocentesis were explained, it began to feel like we were being forced to watch a bad foreign horror film. We didn't know the language, the scenery was all wrong, the actors robotic, and the price of admission unfathomable—our child's life. It felt like our exit was blocked, so escaping before the final credits rolled was not an option.

The professionals informed us that our unborn child had a genetic abnormality called Ring 22, a very rare genetic defect with only thirty-six reported cases in the world. With the information they had gathered, the head geneticist rattled off the conclusion: "This will not be a life worth saving. Your child will be born with severe-to-profound mental retardation as well as too many physical abnormalities to mention. Most reported cases result in an early death due to failure to thrive. There is no use in performing the intrauterine surgery."

The theater seemed to go black. There was no picture, but the sound kept working. The advice given to us was to head back to the suburbs, schedule an appointment with our physician, and wait for our child to die. He would likely be stillborn from kidney failure, since his kidneys were being badly damaged each day due to his malfunctioning valve.

Suddenly, I could barely breathe. I felt like I was being strangled. I looked to my husband with pleading, desperate eyes, silently screaming, *Do something.*

Jerry asked the doctors about inducing labor in order to stop the damage and save our unborn child's life. They told us if they did deliver him early, he might live.

That sounded like good news to us. But, once again, we were told it would be best not to intervene because "this will not be a life worth saving." The physicians advised us to let nature take its course and start planning a funeral. Again, I wondered why I had not miscarried earlier in the pregnancy. As hard as that scenario would have been to deal with, this one was so much worse.

The available research on Ring 22 was placed in a skinny manila folder for Jerry and me to take home, read, and digest. Obtaining information over the internet was a rather new concept in 1983, and with a genetic abnormality as rare as Ring 22, information was sketchy even through the most up-to-date medical journals. The medical team gave us all the information they possessed.

We left the conference room in silence. As the elevator traveled down to the main floor, once again in seeming slow motion, we walked out the door we had entered hours earlier. My heart was heavy, my eyes cast downward.

Jerry stopped suddenly, grabbing my hand. "Ann, look up." Looking at Jerry, I could see his eyes brimming with tears, as were mine. "Look at the sky," he whispered, pointing west.

Through our cloudy eyes, we witnessed a brilliant Texas sunset, taking the place of the overcast sky that had been our companion earlier. Light pierced through our darkness. There was beauty in the midst of our ruin.

That sunset was a sign of hope for us. We felt as though God intentionally put the sunset there for us to focus on him and the beauty he can create in any situation.

From that day forward, we searched for God's light to lead us through our darkest hours. Eyes wide open, looking up, became second nature to us both.

Hope and Confusion

As we left Dallas that day and traveled toward the sunset to our home in the suburbs, Jerry and I agreed to forego the Christmas party we were scheduled to attend. That night sharing (or concealing) the news that our second child would be stillborn was something neither of us could face. Instead, we cocooned with Drew, who was now three, and made plans for the days ahead. First, we needed to see our regular doctor (whom we'll call Dr. Hometown).

The visit with Dr. Hometown brought another shocking revelation. When the doctor asked us what our plans were, Jerry told him, "We're planning a funeral, and when it is all over, I'm taking Ann on a cruise." We had never been on one and probably couldn't afford it, but how in the world does a young couple start recovering from losing a child? Desperate people do desperate things. It sounded like a good-enough plan to us.

Dr. Hometown stared across his desk into our sad eyes. This man had delivered Drew three years earlier, and I had been each year thereafter for a checkup. Including this particular visit, we had seen each other at least six times that year. He was a very kind doctor who always made me feel like I was his most important patient of the day.

What came out of his mouth sent Jerry and me reeling. "What if he lives?"

Silence.

"But the doctors in Dallas and San Francisco say he will die," I countered.

"They are not God," he firmly stated.

God? Jerry and I looked at each other in stunned silence.

We had accepted the grim realization that this child would not make it out of my body alive, and now we were receiving a conflicting message. Having already met with experts in the field of genetics and medicine, we felt we had been given the definitive outcome: Our baby would die.

Or would he?

Dr. Hometown pitched the ultimate curveball; he threw God into the game. Was it *possible* Matthew could live? Was it *possible* the very first doctor we met on Matthew's journey knew that, as a doctor, he was just one of God's instruments? Was it *possible* this was our introduction to one of the scriptures we hung on to throughout Matthew's life? The scripture I'm referring to appears in Matthew 19:26, in which Jesus proclaims, "With God all things are possible."

Our next stop was the Methodist church, where we met with Reverend Kindness. He graciously made room for us on his crowded calendar and greeted us like long-lost friends.

Though Jerry and I were not members, we claimed the church as our home. We had worshiped there on prior occasions, including Christmas, Easter, and sporadic other Sundays.

After sharing the story of my pregnancy and our need to plan a funeral, Reverend Kindness agreed with Dr. Hometown, explaining, "Only God knows the answer. Regardless of whether your baby lives or dies, the church will be here for you."

Waiting

The possibility that our unborn, severely handicapped child could be born alive, struck new chords of distress deep inside our souls. Nothing we had ever done or experienced in our lives had prepared Jerry or me for what lay ahead of us.

Christmas day approached, and, heavy as our hearts were, Jerry and I faced the season with the sense of a new beginning. After visiting with Reverend Kindness, we made a commitment to attend church each week. Our family was whisked on a faith journey beginning that Christmas in 1983. We remembered the birth of Jesus—the real reason for the season. Drew, who had turned three, had his own reason for the season: Santa Claus.

Shortly after the holidays, I developed a cold that seemed to be turning into pneumonia. Trips to Dr. Hometown became more frequent. The nurses listened to my belly with a stethoscope and zeroed in on our baby's faint heartbeat. They shyly smiled when they found it, feeling our pain. We all knew that the damage to Matthew's kidneys was slowly killing him. The doctor had told us that, when the day arrived that a heartbeat could not be detected, they would deliver our dead son.

Three weeks into January 1984, I felt lethargic and feverish, the cold moving from my head to my chest. Jerry somehow heard my silent cries of despair as I wondered when this ordeal would end because, on January 21, he presented me with a precious present that helped ease my pain and suffering. It was the Revised Standard Version of the Holy Bible.

Looking for the wisdom, comfort, and answers I had been told it contained, I tore through the pages. Growing up, my family did not have Bibles lying around the house. Nor did we attend any church regularly. Instead, we jumped around, trying to find a denomination where my father felt comfortable.

He had been raised a strict Catholic in a poor coal-mining town in Pennsylvania. When he and my mother fell in love, Daddy took her to meet the priest and asked him to officiate at their wedding. Mom had been raised Presbyterian. The priest said, "Go back out and find a nice Catholic girl, and then I'll perform the ceremony."

Well, Daddy went out all right, and said that if God felt that way he didn't want any part of the church. They found a Methodist minister who agreed to marry them, and they had a proper wedding ceremony. Mom, a great woman of faith, never gave up trying to get Daddy to church and, at times, succeeded, especially when my brother and I came along. I categorize myself as having grown up a C & E (Christmas and Easter) Christian.

Jerry was raised in the Methodist Church, where his father taught adult Sunday school and served as a lay leader. But, like many young folks, he had fallen away. When Jerry proposed to me, neither of us had a church to call our own. There was a Methodist church in the town where we lived, and, after a few visits, the pastor agreed to marry us.

Proverbs 22:6 says, "Train a child in the way he should go, and when he is old he will not turn from it." Jerry is one of the children this scripture defines. He remembered the book to turn to in times of need. The Bible he gave me that day, signed, *With Love, Jerry & Andrew, 1-21-84,* remains the most precious present he has ever given me.

Years later, I began referring to Jerry as "my other rock." This reference stems from Psalm 18:2, where David says, "The Lord is my rock." Throughout the book of Psalms, David characterizes God's care with symbols, and one of them is a rock that can't be moved by anyone who would harm us. Jerry is my other rock.

The Time Had Come

On January 24, 1984, Dr. Hometown decided to induce labor because I was getting sicker and sicker. He sent me home from my appointment that day to pack a bag and prepare for Matthew to "be taken" the next day.

The godmother-to-be (GTB) met me at the house with Drew. He had spent the day at her house with his best buddy and his buddy's two older brothers. She took one look at me and decided I wasn't going to wait until the next day to go back to the hospital. Instead, she called another neighbor to take over babysitting Drew so she could take me to the hospital that instant.

I was so sick I couldn't even argue. Nor did I want to. Not only did my chest and stomach hurt from the terrible cough I had; there persisted a piercing pain in my back.

When the next-door neighbor came over to watch Drew, her eyes grew wide as she stared at me. She was a registered nurse, and surmised that I was in labor. GTB was pressed into an emergency situation. If three boys under the age of ten had managed to teach their mother one thing, it was how to get to the hospital emergency room *fast.*

As we approached the stoplight where we were supposed to turn left, instead of getting in line, GTB veered to the right, rolled down her window, and started waving her arms and screaming to the cars beside her "Let me cut in front of you. This woman's having a baby!" I felt like I was going to throw up all over her van.

The cars got out of the way, GTB hit the gas, and we sped along. "I've always wanted to say that," she said as she giggled nervously, keeping one eye on the road and the other on me.

In the meantime, somebody had managed to find Jerry. He was in sales, and sometimes had five different stores to stop at in one day. This was long before cell phones were standard accessories, so finding him was our first miracle of the day. He was instructed to get to the hospital—fast.

When I arrived at the hospital, they quickly determined I was in hard labor and could deliver at any minute. It felt nothing like the labor with Drew. Jerry has always reminded me that when I was in labor with Drew, people could hear me screaming for morphine through the halls. I was proof that natural childbirth is not for everyone.

This time was different, though. It seemed like everyone around me was screaming for something, while tried to escape the fact that the end was coming. Before I knew what was happening, I was in a delivery room, surrounded by doctors, nurses, and GTB. A nurse had thrown a gown at her since Jerry wasn't there yet, and invited her into the delivery room.

There were too many voices, too many faces, and I was exhausted and in excruciating pain from the coughing. I closed my eyes, waiting for everything to stop. When I opened them again, Jerry appeared.

Within a matter of seconds, we were looking at Matthew, who arrived quietly into the world on January 24, 1984. There were no flailing arms or legs and no crying, yet he was breathing on his own. That was the second miracle of the day.

We touched him, looked into his eyes, and said our goodbyes. He was whisked away.

God Has the Ultimate Plan

"For I know the plans I have for you"
declares the Lord, "plans to prosper you
and not to harm you, plans to give you
hope and a future."

-Jeremiah 29:11

A New Day

The funeral we planned in 1984 did not take place. Matthew lived. Matthew was a miracle, and Miracle Man became one of his precious nicknames.

However, Matthew was either diagnosed with something new each passing year, or his damaged kidneys, defective heart, and curved spine all worsened. We heard over and over again the devastating news from a doctor that he may not survive his most recent medical challenge. Jerry and I were haunted by the same question we faced when I was pregnant with him: *How in the world do you watch your child die?* The answer we discovered is, you don't. You watch your child live, however long that may be.

The Cancer

Drew discovered Matthew's rare form of cancer while home on a visit from his freshman year at college; Matthew was fifteen. Together they walked through the kitchen, and Drew said, "Mom, you've got to feel this."

As Drew and I felt around, Matthew watched, wiggled, and laughed. There, on the inside of Matthew's forearm, was something that felt like a frozen pea. I wondered if it was just a clogged pore, like a big pimple or boil, that would go away in a few days. Matthew had many health issues that somehow resolved themselves if given a little time.

Drew, playing the overprotective big brother, insisted I take Matthew to the doctor. I hesitated because, by this time, we had become regulars at doctors' offices and hospitals. The sitcom *Cheers* comes to mind, with the part of the jingle that says, "where everybody knows your name."

However, it was fall, and time for Matthew's annual flu shot, so I took that opportunity to have a doctor look at his arm. Again, Matthew squirmed and giggled as his skinny, long arm was poked and prodded. "It's a cyst; nothing to worry about," stated the pediatrician.

Great, I thought. I could cross that off my list of concerns with Matthew; he had other medical challenges attacking his fragile body.

Rotating Knees

Several months before we discovered the cyst on Matthew's arm, his knee became dislocated on quite a few occasions. At times it was incredibly painful for Mattie (another nickname he acquired), making it impossible for him to stand and walk. Lifting and moving him became more challenging for Jerry and me, now that he weighed around 110 pounds. We prayed his knee would heal, enabling him to walk once again. How long would we physically be able to care for him if he were unable to walk? This concern always lurked in the back of our minds.

Walking was one of Matthew's greatest joys. He took his first independent step when he was seven years old, and, once he did walk, he made up for lost time. When we stood him up, he walked and walked and walked, sometimes in circles, with a grin as wide as the Grand Canyon. He was like the Energizer bunny with his robotic, uncoordinated gait and clapping hands.

There was never any rhyme or reason to when his knees became dislocated. One evening, shortly after tucking him into bed, I heard him making noises, which wasn't unusual. Then I heard moaning, which suddenly took on a different, eerie pitch. I went to check and found him lying in bed with his leg at a ninety-degree angle, exactly perpendicular to the way a normal leg should bend at the knee. His contorted face told me he was in incredible pain.

Jerry quickly joined me, and we tugged to get Matthew's long, skinny leg to line up straight again, like Matthew's orthopedic physician (Dr. Good Guy) had previously instructed us to do. On that particular evening, once we got him straightened out, he fell asleep.

At this point in Matthew's life, we had stopped panicking when presented with a medical crisis, especially late in the evening. If he wasn't crying uncontrollably, throwing up nonstop, or running an extremely high temperature, we always tried to wait until the morning to get to a hospital or doctor's office. It was less traumatic for him as well as for Jerry and me. At the end of a long day, a few hours of sleep gave us the energy and clear minds required to make the best decisions regarding medical treatments and options for Matthew.

Early the next morning, before the doctor's office opened, we were in the emergency room. Matthew awoke at 6:00 a.m. (instead of his normal 8:00 a.m.) in more pain, and with a knee the size of a small Nerf basketball.

After explaining to the emergency room nurses what had happened to Matthew, the doctor on call, whom we had never seen before, approached us. The nurse had briefed him in another room. His face grim, he crossed his arms over his chest. "Mr. and Mrs. Joyner, it is impossible for someone's leg to become dislocated while lying in bed."

What was he saying? I looked at Jerry then back to Dr. Suspicious, and repeated what I had told the nurses about the previous night. He was silent. It slowly dawned on me. Here was a nonverbal, severely handicapped teenager, and the doctor had concluded Matthew was being abused. Looking around, I saw no staff in the emergency room who knew Matthew, Jerry, or me. It was obvious we needed someone who could vouch for our integrity as good and loving parents.

Worried and saddened, I wanted to put my hands in front of me for him to place the handcuffs on and say, "Just make sure the cell you take me to is padded and blue!" This was always a joke with our friends who also had handicapped children because things often seemed to happen with our children that were very hard to explain.

For example, one of Matthew's longtime friends, who rode with him on the same bus each day and attended the same school for children with special needs, showed up one morning with his leg in a full cast.

"What in the world happened to Happy Guy?" I asked.

"You'll have to talk to his mom," the driver and assistant said in unison.

Tripping over my own two feet, I ran back into the house to make the call to his mother, Ultimate Patience.

"What in the world happened to Happy Guy?" I blurted out before she could even say hello.

"You are not going to believe this," she said. *Try me*, I thought.

Ultimate Patience went on to tell me how she had securely tucked her child into his second-floor bedroom for the evening. She proceeded to take a long, hot shower in her master bathroom on the first floor. Before turning in for the evening, she walked to the kitchen, passing through the front hallway.

With his nose pressed against the windowpane next to the front door, looking in from the outside, the sight of Happy Guy stopped his mother's heart. He had crawled to that place after falling out of his second-story window. Normally locked and secure, the latch on the window had somehow loosened.

Even though in our heads, we could understand why we

were sometimes questioned by strangers, it never failed to break our hearts. My friends and I would all walk barefoot on hot coals to prevent any harm or suffering from coming to our children.

The morning after Matthew dislocated his knee, I had the feeling Dr. Suspicious had the cops standing on the other side of the door, waiting to haul me away. I was hurt, furious, tired, and concerned about Mattie. "Just call Dr. Good Guy," I managed to whisper, fighting back the tears.

Dr. Suspicious contacted Dr. Good Guy, who assured this skeptical man that if anyone could dislocate a knee while just lying in bed, turning from side to side or front to back, it was Matthew. His body was like a rubber band; born with hypotonia, he had little muscle tone or tension in his body and ligaments. X-rays verified that his kneecaps were basically floating around, with little tissue or muscle holding them down.

"Well, I'm sorry I doubted your story." The apology slipped out of Dr. Suspicious's mouth.

At that moment, I prayed he learned a valuable lesson from my family, one he had obviously failed to learn in medical school: Things are not always as they seem, especially in the world of a handicapped patient.

Dr. Suspicious said surgery would probably be required to screw the kneecap into place. We were sent home with a splint, an ice pack, pain medication, and instructions to make an appointment with Dr. Good Guy.

Discovery and Despair

Matthew and I went to see Dr. Good Guy five times over the next two months. Miraculously, his knees behaved themselves and did not dislocate for those two months. We discussed surgery, but due to all of Matthew's other health issues, including his bad heart and kidneys, the doctor and I agreed to take a wait-and-see approach.

At the end of what was to be our last visit, I asked the doctor to take a quick look at Matthew's arm. I thought the frozen pea had grown since Drew had first discovered it four months earlier. Plus, Matthew no longer smiled when we poked and prodded. In fact, when we even got close to it, he winced and pull his arm back.

While the doctor assured me he thought it was just a cyst, he wanted to take it out, since it was obviously growing and sitting on a nerve. I wondered if I had caused the cyst by grabbing him by the forearm more than a million times to help him to a standing position.

We scheduled outpatient surgery for the following week. Quick and simple, we were told we would be in and out of the hospital in a few hours. Jerry and I had not made a big deal out of it to our church family, friends, or relatives because we weren't worried. It was just another bump in the road—or, in this case, a bump in the arm—for Matthew.

The surgery ended up taking much longer than anticipated. When Dr. Good Guy came out to find us in the waiting room, he looked troubled and confused. Basically all he said was, "That was sure ugly. We've sent it to pathology, and I'll be calling you with the results."

And that was it. Jerry and I tried to question him further, but a nurse appeared, inviting us to join Matthew in recovery.

The call came the very next day, Saturday, from Dr. Good Guy. His voice was barely recognizable as he told us that the frozen pea was a very rare form of cancer. He had contacted a good friend of his who was an orthopedic oncologist to consult on the case. This specialist would call us directly as soon as he returned from his son's basketball game.

Jerry and I looked at each other and tried to remember the last time a doctor had called us on a weekend. That's when you know you're in real trouble. Dread and despair crept into our world.

When the call came an hour or so later, the sunny winter day changed into a dark, frigid night filled with black ice. Epithelioid sarcoma—a rare, aggressive, soft tissue tumor-was the diagnosis. More surgery would be needed, and the possibility of amputating Matthew's left forearm was mentioned by this new doctor, the orthopedic oncologist.

When Drew had turned sixteen three years earlier, we worried about cars, grades, friends, curfews, and employment. Matthew had just turned sixteen, but now we faced the possibility of a child losing a limb or his life. It made our concerns about Drew seem to have been petty.

The night we found out Matthew had cancer, Jerry and I struggled to keep each other from falling through the ice. We had somehow skated through sixteen years with Miracle Man but not on black ice like this. It was dark and cold, and difficult to see God's light.

After crying and holding onto each other for hours that Saturday evening, Jerry and I started making phone calls to tell everyone we knew that Matthew was in need of prayers. It never ceases to amaze us how far and wide our requests for prayer stretch. The message was carried around the country and the world.

God's light began to pierce through our darkness once again. We heard words of comfort and encouragement that night that kept us from falling through the ice.

We wondered, *Is another miracle out there for our blessed Mattie?*

The Treatment

Radiation was the plan. This would be the least traumatic and least invasive course of treatment for Matthew's cancer. My first reaction was, "No! I won't put Matthew through that." Jerry begged me to at least give it a try.

The orthopedic oncologist, Dr. Changed Heart, after struggling with a *go-all-the-way, do-whatever-it-takes-to-cure-*

my-patients-of-cancer attitude, had a change of heart. He
realized further surgery for this cancer was not the answer for
Matthew. Without an arm, Matthew would lose the ability to
walk, which gave him tremendous joy. His raised arms kept
him upright, much like the pole a tightrope walker uses.

When Jerry and I could get doctors to step back and
look at "the whole child," they saw Matthew with the same
eyes we did. The *quality,* not the *quantity,* of Matthew's life
was at the forefront of all of our decisions. Dr. Changed Heart
learned how to step back, something he admitted he had not
been taught in medical school.

We ruled out chemotherapy since this particular cancer did
not usually respond to it, nor would Matthew's heart be able
to tolerate it. Dr. Changed Heart informed us that if Matthew
received no treatment, he would most certainly die within a
year. We asked him what he would do if Matthew were his
child, and he said he would do radiation.

I reluctantly agreed to the recommended therapy. I knew
in my heart it would be impossible for a child like ours to
receive radiation. Matthew was not capable of following
directions or lying still, which are two key components to
successful radiation. How was this going to work?

Giving Matthew sedation each day was not an option due
to his compromised heart and kidneys. I knew he would
probably become hysterical if he were strapped down and left
alone in an unfamiliar room, which is what we were being
asked to do. It would be heartbreaking for us and cruel to
him to suffer through this for six weeks. There was no way to
explain to Matthew that this treatment was for his own good
because his comprehension level never scored above that of a
three-year-old. I was adamant that the minute he cried or got
upset, the treatments would end.

Such was my plan. I knew he would be uncooperative
and miserable. And then, I would have to put a stop to the
radiation treatment. After all, I was his mom; I knew him

better than anyone else in the world, and I knew what was best for him. All I wanted was for Matthew to be happy, whether it was for just one more day, one more week, or one more year. Throughout the years, the doctors also had strong feelings that they knew what was best for Matthew. Jerry could see both sides. I was too stubborn.

Sometimes, though, Matthew's all-knowing and well-meaning mom, and all-knowing and well-meaning doctors, would forget *who* had the ultimate plan: "For I know the plans I have for you," declares the Lord, "plans to prosper you, and not to harm you, plans to give you hope and a future" (Jeremiah 29:11).

Staging

The radiation treatment for Matthew's cancer began in the middle of winter in the year 2000. Staging was the first step in the course of radiation. Maybe they call it that because it feels like play practice; lights were set, props were built, the music score was chosen, and actors in all shapes and sizes showed up for the opening. The star of the show was our Matthew. Ironically, our first introduction to Matthew had felt like a play as well.

Jerry and I, who became the directors, shared all our fears and concerns with the supporting actors. While they were absolutely wonderful at their jobs, everyone quickly realized Matthew was not their normal leading man, and were unsure of the best approach. He was unable to communicate with anyone, at least verbally. Each person involved knew there was everything to gain if we could make radiation therapy work and everything to lose if it did not. Fortunately, they were willing to listen and learn about their newest patient from Jerry and me. No class had been offered to teach them about handicapped individuals receiving radiation therapy.

We shared about how Matthew was unlike other people when it came to his reaction to pain or discomfort. The reaction was almost always delayed. When he was a baby receiving his inoculations, he would sometimes laugh and giggle during and after receiving a shot. The attitudes of the nurse and the person holding him down—usually Jerry or me—were the key. If you could keep smiling, he would smile back, even through the pain. Tears may have sprung up in his eyes, but, more often than not, that is where they stayed. Little pools magnified his big, brown, questioning eyes.

This reaction was a blessing and a curse throughout the years as Matthew endured numerous surgeries and illnesses. He could be in incredible pain, and we didn't necessarily know it. For instance, one time he had a burst eardrum. He had been laughing for days while he had a very severe ear infection. Unfortunately, we had not picked up on that. It was usually only when his temperature reached 101 degrees or he didn't stop crying that we loaded up the car to head to a doctor's office or the hospital.

The first day we staged for radiation was a hoot. I remember fearfully entering the hospital with Jerry and Matthew and proceeding to a bank of elevators. The minute the door closed and the elevator started to descend to the basement of the hospital, Matthew started to laugh, rocking back and forth in his wheelchair, and slapping his hands together in his uncoordinated clap. Jerry and I looked at each other and could not help but smile.

Matthew was in his own little world, and at times like this, that was a blessing. He had no idea where we were going or what we were going to do. I told myself to keep smiling and lifted a silent prayer to God that everyone we encountered that day would be able to do the same.

From the minute we stepped off the elevator, it was evident that everyone involved in Matthew's treatment had thoroughly read the script and was prepared to support their leading man. Doctors, nurses, and radiation technicians approached the wheelchair with smiles planted firmly in place as the required costume, so to speak. With a song in their voices, they each greeted Matthew, excitedly calling him by name and touching him. Matthew loved all the attention and smiled back.

A technician escorted us to the stage, the room where the radiation would be delivered. Jerry and I lifted Matthew out of his wheelchair and placed him on a very large table, which he immediately tried to scoot off. Stagehands started to scurry about, coming up with every prop at their disposal, to secure Mr. Mattie to his perch.

Large Velcro straps bound Matthew to the table; one across the ankles, another around the middle of his thigh, yet another at his waist, and one across his chest. We placed extra padding under his body to cushion his spine—which had been fused five years earlier due to severe scoliosis—against the cold metal table. At this point, it was Jerry's and my eyes that brimmed with tears, not Matthew's. His were bright, smiling, and shining, looking at all his new friends and surroundings.

Another technician carefully placed Matthew's left arm out to his side, as far away from his body as they could get it. The radiation was meant for his forearm, nothing else. They needed to protect his damaged heart and kidneys. That first day, they molded his arm inside a plaster-of-Paris type of mesh material. It was cut away, like a cast would be, and stored on a shelf in the room. Each subsequent time we went in for radiation, the cast sat waiting on the table. They inserted his arm into this contraption then secured it to the adjacent table.

Every part of Matthew's body was strapped down, except for his right arm and head. His head could move from side to side without affecting anything, and he could bring his right hand to his mouth, which was a habit he developed soon after birth. It was our hope and prayer that this bit of freedom would be enough to satisfy Mattie.

Practice continued, with the spotlights being shone on the star. When the lights came up, Matthew was mesmerized. Tiny, bright-green beams came from all around the room. It looked like *Star Wars*. This laser show brought squeals of laughter from Matthew.

More giggles erupted as the stage moved from side to side and up and down to achieve just the right angle on the cancer. Maybe he thought he was on a ride in an amusement park; we had no way of knowing. Whatever he thought, it was becoming apparent that this treatment was an exciting and fun adventure for Matthew, rather than the scary, dreadful experience I thought it would be.

The Production

After several days of staging, it was time for our leading man to do his solo. Everyone, including Jerry and me, had to leave the room. As I watched the thick, steel-and-concrete door close, my throat began to close with it. I had a fear that something would malfunction and we wouldn't be able to get the door open. Matthew would be alone.

Upon exiting the room, we could see and hear Matthew, thanks to audio and video monitors. For the next six weeks, we stood with the technicians at every appointment, watching the screens and hearing the audio. He was never out of our sight. It took several treatments for me to be as relaxed and trusting as Matthew was, and to smile even when he wasn't looking at me.

Matthew picked up a new name of Houdini during the course of his radiation. Occasionally, Mattie wiggled out of a strap right after the door closed and before the radiation was administered, necessitating a cut in the action. The actors all rushed back to center stage and got their main man ready to reshoot the scene. All the attention seemed pleasing to Matthew. He really got a kick out of it.

The musical score I chose for the play came from Disney's

movie *Tarzan*. It began playing the instant we placed him on the table. *Tarzan* was one of Mattie's favorite movies. Each time he watched it, it was like the first time, bringing smiles and laughter. I had heard the soundtrack from the movie many times before, but it was the first day of treatment when the words to one song, "You'll Be in My Heart," by Phil Collins, hit home. It is the second song on the soundtrack. In particular, a few lines stand out:

> *I will protect you*
> *From all around you*
> *I will be here*
> *Don't you cry*
>
> *For one so small,*
> *You seem so strong*
> *My arms will hold you,*
> *Keep you safe and warm*
> *This bond between us can't be broken*
> *I will be here*
> *Don't you cry*

Ultimately, I realized Matthew was never alone in that room. I believed God was present, perhaps standing by his side, holding his hand and smiling down at him. Or, perhaps God lay next to him on the table, with his arms gently trying to hold our squirming little man as still as possible. Maybe that was the reason Matthew didn't become hysterical, and I didn't have to step in and halt the treatment. That's the only explanation I have for why it worked.

Between the music, lights, sounds, and fabulous actors, the play managed to keep Matthew's attention and ran for the entire six-week engagement. It was an adventure that, for the most part, kept him happy.

The extras also played a big part. These were all the other people who came for their radiation treatment, usually for some type of cancer. At first, we tried to avoid them because they all looked sad and sick. Friends and pastors advised me to put the blinders on each day we went for radiation therapy.

This is part of the armor many parents of sick children carry around. The blinders help you stay focused on your own child. But as the treatments wore on, fellow patients and their families, whom we met in the halls and waiting rooms, began responding to Matthew's smiles and odd, happy behavior. They smiled back and asked me what his story was.

I vividly remember speaking with a woman who was in the waiting room one day. She rarely smiled, but on this particular day she beamed. "It is Matthew who keeps me coming back day after day," she confessed. "If he can do it, so can I."

Suddenly, more and more people began to share the positive impact Matthew had on them. Matthew showed up for radiation each day with at least two escorts, usually Jerry and me, or sometimes a friend joined me if Jerry couldn't. The doors of the elevator opened into the cold basement of the hospital where the radiation department was, and Matthew's giggles echoed down through the halls, warming the hearts of everyone within earshot.

The blinders came off in the hospital, and I could see. I saw Matthew encourage and inspire the people around him to do things they didn't think were possible. This was just one of the incredible gifts God gave our severely handicapped, sick child.

Amazingly, he did this without ever saying a single word.

Eyes Wide Open

"Open My Eyes, That I May See" is the hymn of encouragement that gave me the confidence to abandon the blinders and continue to seek out God's ultimate plan for our family. Difficult as it is to look beyond a certain moment or day, the future calls us to see God's will.

With Matthew's chaotic radiation ordeal barely behind us, our family experienced chaos in other areas as well. The company Jerry worked for was being reorganized, and he was offered a position in Los Angeles. This would be the third move in seven years' time—first Kansas City then Denver—and the thought of it happening so soon after Matthew's bout with cancer depressed us. We were comfortable in our church, our medical community, and in the blanket of love and security friends had thrown around us.

The thought of being unemployed and without insurance, with thousands of dollars of medical bills mounting daily, terrified us. There was no other offer on the table, though; therefore, he reluctantly accepted.

Jerry started commuting during the summer of 2000. He explained to his boss that Matthew was too weak from the six-plus weeks of radiation to undertake a move before the fall. He needed time to heal. The company graciously accepted the fact I would be staying behind for several months and allowed Jerry to travel back and forth between Los Angeles and Denver.

It is said that things happen in threes, and so it was with our family: Matthew's radiation had barely ended; the move to California loomed. Drew just completed his freshman year at the University of Northern Colorado. He suddenly felt called to move back to Kansas City, where we lived before moving to Colorado.

At first, I thought his timing was terrible. But Jerry's job was taking us to California, so maybe this would be for the best. We had people in Kansas City who cared for Drew and our family deeply. One of those people was his old youth pastor and friend, Mentor Man, who was in the middle of building a house. He and Drew worked out a plan to finish the basement together, which would provide an inexpensive and safe place for Drew to live. Jerry and I had worked with

Mentor Man years earlier as youth sponsors at our church, and we thought the world of him.

Drew would be living in a familiar place with a terrific role model; his future looked bright. Jerry and I were not feeling as optimistic about our future in California with Matthew. We spent hours on the computer researching the medical community, the housing market, and schools for Matthew in California. With each new Google search, we were disheartened. But we saw no better alternative, so we forged ahead.

The plan was to get Drew relocated and settled before we moved. Jerry took some vacation time, packed all of Drew's worldly possessions, and headed down the highway to Kansas City with him. Traveling Interstate 70 between Colorado and Kansas can be a very boring, tedious drive, with time to do some heavy thinking and praying. With the past disappearing in the rearview mirror, my dear husband thought about our future.

I received a call from him several hours into the trip. "You would hate to know there was a billion-dollar lottery out there, and you had not bought a ticket, and you may have had a chance to win, wouldn't you?"

He was rambling, and I panicked. Had he taken our savings and bought a bunch of lottery tickets, hoping to win so we wouldn't have to move to California? Had my solid-as-a-rock husband finally succumbed to the pressure of raising a medically challenged, severely handicapped son, and lost his mind?

"What are you saying?" I shouted.

Jerry sensed my anxiety, panic, and stress, and quit with the analogy of buying a lottery ticket. He said he was thinking of making a call to an old friend in Kansas City and inviting him to lunch. Jerry heard that his business had taken off, and, although it was a long shot, thought maybe he could go to work for him.

Jerry purchased the imaginary lottery ticket and won. He accepted a job the next day in Kansas City and left the company that had been planning to move us to California. I was relieved, since we felt like Kansas City was home. We had our old church home, friends, doctors, and hospitals that were all familiar to us. Plus, Drew was already there.

Hadn't I questioned Drew's timing just a few months before? It appeared, once again, that God had the ultimate plan, and if we kept our eyes wide open, he would show us the way.

Preparing To Move

The day I told Dr. Changed Heart we would be leaving Denver to move to Kansas City, I discovered how attached he had gotten to Matthew in six short months. The doctor told me he would have to search the Kansas City area to see if there was someone capable of taking over Matthew's case because he needed to be followed closely. I got the feeling Dr. Changed Heart thought he was the only orthopedic oncologist who knew exactly what to do for our precious guy. Matthew had succeeded not only in changing his heart but in stealing and melting it as well.

Jerry and Drew were in Kansas City completing the move into Mentor Man's house. It was a stressful week, with Drew's departure and Jerry's acceptance of another job. I longed to get Matthew tucked away in bed so I could have some downtime to process all that had happened. The evenings were always a challenge when I was alone with Matthew. I was usually tired at the end of the day, and bathing him was like an aerobic workout with an octopus. He weighed more than one hundred pounds, was slippery when wet, his arms and legs flew everywhere, making me think and feel like he had five sets of each.

Since Jerry and Drew knew of the nightly routine, they held off calling me until after eight o'clock. Around seven,

Matthew was sitting on the toilet, squealing at the sound and sight of running water in the bathtub. The phone rang, and though I was tempted not to answer, I felt drawn to it.

After saying a quick hello, I heard, "Ann–what are you doing?"

Certain it was Jerry, I shouted something sarcastic like, "What do you think I'm doing?"

Then this guy answered excitedly, "Wait, wait, I've got to pull off the road again."

It suddenly dawned on me that this wasn't Jerry's voice on the other end. While whoever it was on the phone pulled off to the side of the road, I quickly turned off Matthew's bathwater and left the bathroom, knowing he couldn't get up by himself and would be fine sitting a bit longer on the toilet. He wore diapers all the time, but we had some success on the toilet as well.

"This is Doctor Changed Heart. You are not going to believe what I have to tell you. I think you should sit down." He was now pulled off to the side of the road, but he was talking sixty miles per hour. "I was just on my way home from the hospital, and I received a call from Nurse Angel, the doctor's assistant in Kansas City, who I called early this morning. I explained to her how I am treating this 16-year-old boy for epitheliod sarcoma when this woman interrupted me. She eagerly exclaimed, 'You are talking about Matthew Joyner.' I almost drove off the road! She went on to tell me she knew Matthew well, having met him at church several years before."

I sat on the couch with tears falling freely down my cheeks. Nurse Angel was actually one of Matthew's first angel care workers at our church in Kansas City, where Matthew's Ministry began in 1993. The night Matthew was diagnosed with cancer in Denver, we cried out for prayers. The next morning, our dear friend and former Kansas City pastor, Adam Hamilton, asked the congregation to join him in praying for Matthew. Nurse Angel was at that service. She had gone to work for the head of the Sarcoma Institute in Kansas City years earlier.

Dr. Changed Heart blurted out, "What are the chances?" Although he didn't come out and say it, I could tell by his voice that he knew, as we did, that someone else was in charge of Matthew's destiny: The Spirit was definitely at work in all of our lives.

3 Amazing Goodness

"And we know that in all things, God works for the good of those who love him." -Romans 8:28

Running the Race

A marathon is described as any contest or event of great or greater-than-normal length or duration; something that requires exceptional endurance. Cancer is a grueling marathon, requiring exceptional endurance of everyone involved. The people you select to be on your team are vital.

Pie Lady and I met at a church auction where Jerry and I held the winning bid for her pie-a-month for one year. It was shortly after our first introduction that I found out not only did this woman create mouth-watering pies and other culinary delights; she was known for creating plenty of food for thought as well.

His Timing

A few weeks after Matthew completed his radiation treatments and was back at school, Pie Lady and I met for lunch. Her best friend had died of cancer three years earlier, and, although Pie Lady had several good girlfriends, none could fill the void Paula had left.

After I pulled into a parking spot, I spotted my friend as I got out of my car.

"Perfect timing!" I yelled to her.

We hugged and walked together to the entrance of the restaurant. *Something has changed since my last visit here*, I thought. *What is that white awning for?* The closer we got to the door, the posters and signs lining the tables became legible:

The American Cancer Society Relay for Life.

A perky, young woman stood behind the table shouting in rapid-fire succession: "Are you two familiar with Relay for Life? Would you like to sign up? Do you have any questions?"

Pie Lady answered, "Yes. Yes, I am familiar with it. My best friend died from cancer."

Oh, great, I thought. *Our lunch is ruined. Now all we will be able to think about is Paula, Matthew, and the awful disease they have been struck with—cancer.*

Not deterred in the least, Miss Perky continued. "Well then, you certainly know firsthand the importance of finding a cure for cancer. Would you consider forming a team in your friend's memory?"

"Let me get back to you on that," my friend said curtly as she grabbed my elbow and ushered me into the restaurant.

Our usual chattiness abandoned us as we dined. We were deep in our own thoughts about our loved ones and about cancer. Everywhere I went, it seemed like there was a reminder that cancer was now a part of Matthew's life. I could not escape it, even for a quick lunch.

As we were about to leave the restaurant, Pie Lady announced, "I've been sitting here thinking you and I are being called to do something for Paula and Matthew."

"What do you mean? Who is calling us?" I replied, knowing where the conversation was headed.

"Don't you get it, Ann? You know as well as I do that God places things in our path. It is up to us to take notice. I think there is a reason they are advertising Relay for Life here today. We need to form a team in memory of Paula and in honor of Matthew to raise funds that will help find a cure for cancer. That's what we're supposed to do." My friend smiled now, sure of what she was being called to.

I shook my head slowly from side to side, eyes closed, thinking: *God, I need a rest. Has everyone forgotten that I just completed six weeks of exhausting radiation treatments with my handicapped son? What about Matthew 11:28, where you say, "Come to me, all you who are weary and burdened, and I will give you rest"? Surely*, I thought, *I am being called to rest alongside Matthew.*

Pie Lady took two registration packets from Miss Perky as we exited the restaurant, and placed one in my hand. "Read all the information and give me a call tomorrow. We need to get started. The relay is only three weeks away."

Later that same evening, curled up in a chair, I reluctantly read all the literature in the packet from The American Cancer Society describing Relay for Life. It is an eighteen-hour team relay event to raise funds to fight cancer and raise awareness of cancer in the community. The more I read, it sounded like it had the potential of being at least a twenty-four-hour event. That did not include the time I would need to spend organizing and preparing. Conflicting thoughts filled my head. Did I really have the time or energy for this?

If we participate, maybe some good can come out of Matthew and Paula being struck with cancer, I thought. Wasn't that what Pie Lady had said? After debating with myself for what seemed like hours, I found another scripture that evening, which spoke louder than the one I thought was calling me to rest. "And we know that in all things God works for the good of those who love him, who have been called according to his purpose" (Romans 8:28).

Sitting this one out was not an option. My friend was right. We were being called.

Relay for Life

The invitation Pie Lady and I created was persuasive. We encouraged people to join Matthew's Marchers and Paula's Persistent Team in The American Cancer Society's Relay for Life by sharing the four key components of the event.

It's about *hope*: A cancer survivor's celebration and a reflection of the courage and compassion of the people who participate.

It's about *life*: Symbolized by the cancer survivors who walk that first victory lap to kick off the event.

It's about *light*: We light luminaries at dusk to honor our loved ones who have survived cancer, and in memory of those we've lost.

It's about a *cure*: Each of us who takes part in this important event is fighting for a cure together.

The Last Shall Be First

Finally, the day arrived. Matthew's Marchers and Paula's Persistent Team scrambled to find a spot on the infield of the school track. We pitched tents, unfolded lawn chairs, erected food tables, and placed coolers filled with food and drink around the perimeter of our cozy campsite. It would be our home away from home for the next eighteen hours. Six o'clock was minutes away. We could barely hear announcements over the buzz of the crowd.

"Did anyone hear where Matthew and I are supposed to go?" I yelled to our team.

"Over there," I heard in three-part harmony. Several team members pointed to the space next to the band. Their music added to the festive spirit in the air.

My plan was to leave Matthew sitting as long as I could.

Men, women, and children slowly made their way to the start. Although each face was unique, they all shared the same look of determination I had come to recognize in the faces of people receiving treatment for cancer. They were survivors, at least for that day. Just like us, they had come to celebrate.

Suddenly overcome with emotion, I thought, I *cannot do this. I cannot walk Mattie around the track without breaking down.* The tears were ready to flow when Jerry's voice interrupted my thoughts.

"Get Matthew out of his chair!" he shouted from the sideline with the video camera resting on his shoulder. "The race is about to start."

Blinking back the tears, I unbuckled the seatbelt on

Matthew's wheelchair and pushed the footrests to the side. Holding him under the arms, I carefully pulled him to a stand. With as much encouragement as I could muster, I said, "Get your sea legs on, bud, we are going for a long walk."

Cheers went up as the ribbon across the track dropped. Matthew and I were in the front of the pack. Holding him by a belt loop with one hand on one side, I cradled his arm by the elbow on the other. He moved slowly, putting one foot in front of the other, leaning into me.

"Matthew! Matthew! Matthew!"

Jerry, Drew, and our team members called his name, hoping Matthew would look their way so they could snap a picture of him doing his victory lap. Everyone looked fuzzy to me. The tears had pooled in my eyes, and I desperately fought them back. This was, after all, something to smile about.

With the Rocky Mountains in the background and the sun perched slightly above their peaks, God's glorious light splashed across the sky. Looking up, and around at all the people gathered for this event, I saw again how God can, and does, work for good in *all things*. His light does pierce through the darkness.

Matthew slowed down. Other survivors had walked past us, completing their first lap. The only thing in front of us was the finish line, and I spotted the wheelchair off to the side.

"Come on, Mattie. You can make it," I whispered, as much to myself as to him. My arms tingled, almost asleep from balancing his fragile, gangly body. He had not walked this far in months, spending the majority of his time in his wheelchair or lying on the couch.

Matthew looked up, and his crooked smile told me, "I know I can, Mom." With renewed energy and a sense of purpose, I guided us toward our cheering group of supporters. They were getting closer, as was the wheelchair.

Because I was concentrating so hard on getting to the

finish line, I did not see what was happening behind us. The field of competitors had made it around the track a second time, and instead of passing us, they fell in behind, allowing Matthew and me to lead the way. *The last shall be first.* Cheers went up again, and when I caught a glimpse of Jerry, I noticed tears of joy brimming in his eyes as he watched his son cross the finish line.

Illumination

Matthew rode around the track a few more laps in his wheelchair, and then our teammates bid him goodnight as a friend whisked him away so he could spend the night in the soft comforts of his home and bed. The teams he and Paula had inspired planned to stay on the track throughout the evening and into the morning hours to fulfill their commitments.

As the sun set behind the mountains, darkness began to settle in. A flickering light caught my attention across the track as a friend and I took our turn walking several laps. The one light multiplied. Two, then three, four, and so on, until the message was complete on the side of a hill: H-O-P-E. Luminaries glowed, honoring our loved ones who had survived cancer, and in memory of those we'd lost.

Matthew and Paula's teammates raised several thousand dollars that night for cancer research, patient care services, prevention and education, and advocacy. Once again, I was reminded God can wring good out of bad, filling me with *hope*, if I allow him.

The Truth

"The church will be here for you," the words Reverend Kindness had uttered in Texas sixteen years before, were indeed true. The members of the first church in our family's life opened their hearts and arms to us. They surrounded us with prayers, offers to help, words of encouragement, and more. Matthew was two months old when he was well enough to begin attending church with Jerry and me. Everyone who met him knew they were witnesses to a miracle.

As he grew and became stronger, the days he lay quietly in my arms, sleeping through the service, ended. The silent prayer time was no longer silent as Matthew's vocalizations rang out through the sanctuary. In addition, it felt like each time Reverend Kindness tried to drive a point home, Matthew chimed in.

After visiting the church nursery and getting to know the lead volunteers, we decided it was actually possible for someone else to hold Matthew while we worshiped and that he would be fine. It appeared he would fit right in with all the other vocal babies, and receive the extra attention he needed.

Jerry and I became so comfortable with the care he received that we accepted offers to teach children's Sunday school for an extra hour after worship service. I taught third grade, and gained the elementary church education I had not received while growing up. What the children did not know is that I was their equal, soaking up every song, verse, and Bible story as much as they were. I think of them as my first disciple group.

Jerry's experience was not as rewarding as mine, at least not immediately. He had the challenge of teaching sixth graders, who—when given the choice—preferred to sleep until noon on Sunday. One day, I was taking one of my students down the hall to the bathroom when I noticed two of Jerry's students standing outside his door.

"What kind of game was your class playing today?" I asked Jerry on the way home.

"There were no games, just a lesson and group discussion," he said.

"Then why were those two boys standing outside your door?" I asked.

"Ha! I told them to go find their parents. They were being rude, and I had already warned them once, so I asked them to leave," Jerry said matter of factly.

"Jerry," my voice went up two octaves. "You cannot kick students out of your class. This is church. I am on staff. This is not going to go over well at all with Miss Christian Education Director." I was shocked and furious Jerry would act that way, knowing that I was employed by the church, having taken a part-time job as an office assistant, which enabled me to use the skills I had acquired in secretarial college. It was the first real job I had taken since Matthew had been born, and it was perfect; he attended school less than a half mile away.

"Ann, if they did not go to their parents, they obviously knew they were wrong. Stop worrying. My guess is that I got my point across."

I relayed the story to Miss CED the next morning. She replied, "Thank you for the heads up, Ann. Sixth-grade Sunday school has always been a challenge. Finding a teacher who can mentor this age group, and not turn them off to church, is tricky. My gut tells me Jerry may be the leader I have been praying for."

The Spirit did work through Jerry, turning questioning preteens toward God. It was like magic. His class attendance soared, and held events like car washes to raise money for missions. Somehow, he knew exactly what to do with those kids.

Jerry, Drew, and I all grew in our faith as we planted ourselves firmly in the church community.

Back Against the Wall

Our bliss ended when Matthew was three years old. One Sunday, I noticed other moms backing up, holding their small babies close, as I approached the nursery room to drop him off. His vocalizations and size were no longer like those of a new baby. Rather, they were more in line with a temper-tantrum-throwing toddler, especially that day. He was not happy, and let everyone around him know it. Looking at me sympathetically, the nursery worker took him from my arms, trying to defuse a tense situation for all involved.

Matthew no longer fit. He was too fragile to move up with typical two- and three-year-old children, and too menacing-looking to these new moms for him to continue in the nursery. *What now, God?* I wondered. *How can we continue to attend church with Matthew?*

While contemplating our options, I met with Miss CED and other church leaders. When I asked if I could start a program for people with special needs, their initial response was, "We have tried that before."

"Maybe it is time we try it again," I pleaded.

"Ann," Miss CED explained, "a number of years ago there were several young people with special needs here, and we formed a special class. At first there was great enthusiasm, but we did not have families who were committed one hundred percent, and that is what it takes."

"We are committed, and, honestly, there is no longer an appropriate place for Matthew to go on Sunday mornings. He does not fit in, and I know there are more members who feel the same way about their children." (Surely, there had to be.) "I will lead this class and take responsibility," I said with more confidence than I actually had.

Miss CED smiled and suggested I draw up a plan and present it to lead staff the following week.

I had stumbled across a little something called "What Is Life" years earlier. It read like a prescription, and when I followed the directions, I always felt better. As I laid the groundwork for Matthew's special needs class, I kept it in plain sight on my desk. It reads:

Life is a challenge --- meet it
Life is a gift --- accept it
Life is an adventure --- dare it
Life is a sorrow --- overcome it
Life is a tragedy --- face it
Life is a duty --- perform it
Life is a game --- play it
Life is a mystery --- unfold it
Life is a song --- sing it
Life is an opportunity --- take it
Life is a journey --- complete it
Life is a promise --- fulfill it
Life is a beauty --- praise it
Life is a struggle --- fight it
Life is a goal --- achieve it
Life is a puzzle --- solve it

In the first advertisement of the class, I included this little bit of text that has been so encouraging to me, along with the postscript: "Life is truly all of these! It is through the gift of grace that God, and we, help others achieve their glory."

Amazing Grace

Amazing Grace was the name I selected for the class. That hymn was the first song I heard in church when Matthew lay sleeping in my arms one of the first days we attended. Written just for me, or so it felt.

Teaching third grade Sunday school had prepared me for the ten enthusiastic students, ranging in age from three to twenty-eight years old, who enrolled in Amazing Grace. Equipped with a love of music, animation, and crafts, all the students were able to grow in their faith as a committed group of volunteers modified everything to meet each individual's needs. Matthew fit in once again.

Part Two

Becoming an Active Participant

4 VICTIM OR VICTOR?

"Do not neglect the gift that is in you."
- 1 Timothy 4:14, NKJV

Circumstances

The choice was mine. I could leave the church because we no longer fit, or I could stay and build a program for Matthew and others. Although it might have been easier to retreat then and, at other times, to be victimized by life's circumstances, I knew that was not what God had in store for my family and me. God had given me certain gifts that Matthew was exceptional at unwrapping if I allowed. Creating the class Amazing Grace tapped into gifts I was unaware I possessed. The class also revealed the talents that each special participant had been blessed with. It was an amazing venture.

Heads Above Water

Texas has two seasons: hot and not quite as hot. Construction began on the swimming pool in our backyard when Matthew was three months old. Drew was three and a half, and had spent his previous summers at a community pool with his buddies and me. With his frail new brother, Jerry and I knew our days at the community pool were over. So, although putting in a built-in pool may not have been the best financial decision, it turned into one of our best investments.

The pool was like a magnet for all of Drew's friends. Those who came, and stuck by him through the years, were there not only because they liked Drew; they liked and accepted his different brother as well. The same was true for Jerry's and my circle of friends.

Jerry's weekdays were filled with work while I packed

up Matthew each day and headed to doctor visits, therapists, early childhood development sessions, and hospitals. Drew either went to a Mother's Day Out program, a friend's house, or tagged along with Matthew and me. By the time the weekends rolled around, the pool was our oasis, a place to be refreshed with friends, relatives, and each other.

Entertaining was always enjoyable before Matthew entered our lives, and with his addition, we seemed to crave it even more. I quickly discovered that being a parent of a handicapped child was hurtful and isolating at times. It was healthy and helpful to vent with friends.

One day, following a long physical therapy session, Matthew and I stopped by the store on the way home. These sessions, which wore Mattie out, worked on strengthening what little muscle tone he was born with. I put him over my arm, facing forward in his most comfortable position, and into the store we went.

As I scoured a shelf for the needed item, a scream echoed down the aisle. Turning to see what in the world was wrong, I noticed a wide-eyed lady staring at Matthew and me.

"It moved," she hesitantly stammered.

"What moved?" I innocently asked while looking around.

"Hi—Hi—Hi—Him," she croaked out as she pointed to Matthew. "I thought it was a Cabbage Patch Doll."

I grabbed my item, fighting the urge to throw it at Miss Wide Eyes, paid, and left the store as quickly as I could without dropping either Matthew or my purchase. Sitting in the car, trying to stop my hands and insides from shaking, I was not sure whether to laugh or cry. When I glanced in the rear view mirror, I saw my limp little guy sound asleep in his car seat, looking peaceful in his own little world.

As I floated around the pool the next weekend with friends and relayed my encounter with Miss Wide Eyes, they assured me that Matthew was much cuter than any Cabbage Patch Doll they had ever seen. I agreed. He was beautiful.

The Water Kind of Therapy

Water therapy, water aerobics, and water play all help to strengthen the body, not to mention the mind and soul. The summer following Matthew's surgery to close the opening in his stomach, we were finally able to have him in the water, as opposed to lying on a float on top of the water. With a smile splashed across his face, Matthew's flapping arms and kicking legs met the desired resistance to strengthen his muscles. He was extremely happy in the water.

If the pool proved to be a good investment, the water therapist we hired was priceless. Not only did Matthew benefit from this environment; his newfound friends from Early Childhood Development did as well. They each had their turn being guided by the therapist, squealing with glee as their little bodies were totally free, weightless in the water, and able to bend and move in new directions.

For their parents, our pool became an oasis as well, as they came to quench their thirst: a thirst for knowledge, shared frustrations, desired fellowship, and laughter with families who looked just like them. Although I had a chance to visit with a number of the moms at Matthew's school each day, our pool gave the dads and siblings a chance to connect too.

The adult Sunday school class Jerry and I were members of also gravitated to our pool with a couple of parties each summer. The game of choice was covering a watermelon with cooking oil and tossing it to the kids to catch as they jumped off the side of the pool into the water. It provided hours of cheap, fun entertainment for everyone.

Drew scored a home run the day we hosted the pool party marking the end of a tee ball season. Hot dogs on the grill, engraved trophies standing by to be presented, cans of pop overflowing the cooler, and a pool inviting young boys to show off their fierce cannonballs, added up to Drew being the bright and shining star off the field. Mattie hung out on the enclosed patio, safe from the rowdy boys, who turned into gentle young men as they scooted toys within Matthew's reach when they passed through the patio to use the restroom. That day, like many others, we brought the party to us, and everyone won.

Auntie M introduced me to the saying "If Momma ain't happy, ain't nobody happy." The pool made Momma happy.

Perfectly Placed or Misplaced?

Common sense should tell education professionals that placing a nonverbal, severely mentally and physically handicapped person in Spanish or choir class with typical-age peers will not please all parents of handicapped children. In fact, it can turn a perfectly levelheaded and rational person into an unrecognizable being.

"Matthew is in the choir room with the fourth grade class, practicing for the spring concert," I was informed when I stopped by the school one day.

Going through the choir door, I was saddened and infuriated by what I saw. There was Matthew, standing between two of his singing peers, looking off to the side and up at the ceiling, with his hands being held. Not only did he look uncomfortable and out of place; the two helpers were unable to keep up with their singing because Matthew was distracting. After observing for a few minutes, I made my way to the principal's office.

"But most parents want their children with their non-handicapped peers all day," several educators said in unison a week later at the meeting.

"Well, I'm not most parents." I fought to keep my voice from rising. "Besides the fact that Matthew loves music, what is appropriate about what I observed? He has never said a word, let alone sung a tune. He will not focus on the choir director like the other children. He cannot stand for the entire concert. He will not be quiet. You are drawing attention to the fact that he is more disabled than able." I was rambling. "Would it not be more appropriate for Matthew to hand out the programs? This would allow him to work on one of his goals we set up together as a team: *Hold on to an object for five seconds.* This would allow him to be doing something useful and appropriate, within his ability." I was begging at this point.

"That is a great idea, Ann," someone said quietly, sounding a bit embarrassed. "We will start working on that right away."

Matthew only dropped a few programs while handing them out at the spring concert. The recipients were incredibly gracious.

Unannounced visits to Matthew's school always enlightened me. Two years later, at another school, I found him sitting in the back row of a Spanish class. I was told Matthew was being given the English word for every Spanish word spoken. What were they thinking? That maybe Matthew could speak Spanish since he had not picked up English? *Adios* to that placement.

First Steps

The first public school Matthew attended was a segregated campus for students with severe learning disabilities ranging in age from three to twenty-one. At first, this placement terrified Jerry and me. However, in a short while, we were convinced it provided the foundation that gave Matthew the life skills he could not obtain elsewhere.

I received a call from the principal, Miss Steel Magnolia, one morning while I was working at the church a few blocks away. "Ann, I need you to come over. Are you available now?" Miss Steel Magnolia lovingly received her nickname from a few moms serving on the PTA board. MSM had shared with us one evening that having sons and daughters with disabilities made us delicate as magnolias, although inside we were tough as steel. The success and challenge of this segregated school campus turned her into the ultimate steel magnolia.

"Is Matthew okay?" I hurriedly asked.

"Oh, yes, yes. I did not mean to startle you. I just have something I want you to see, and wondered if now would be a good time," she calmly explained.

I was not convinced all was well with our little guy. The staff were masters at getting parents to the school without panicking, only to later reveal the child had had several seizures, was throwing up uncontrollably, or had fallen and required stitches. Greeting me at the door was Miss Steel Magnolia along with a cafeteria worker and maintenance personnel. *This cannot be good*, I thought.

"Good to see you, Ann. Why don't we go visit Matthew's room?" she suggested. I was skeptical about what I was going to find, but all three were smiling, so I relaxed a bit. As we were about to round the corner of the hall leading to Matthew's classroom, Miss Steel Magnolia announced a bit louder, "It really is good to see you, Ann." It dawned on me that I had seen her the day before when I had dropped something by the school. What was she up to?

My three escorts stopped as I turned the corner and nearly fell to my knees. There, before me, was my seven-year-old son, walking unassisted for the first time.

One, two, three, four, five—Matthew saw me, smiled, hesitated, wobbled, and continued—six, seven. He leaned forward into the open arms of the therapist who had been rolling backward on a stool. A teacher stood on one side of Matthew and an assistant on the other, all within inches to catch him if needed. They had let go the minute they heard Miss Steel Magnolia announce my arrival with her "good to see you" line practiced and perfectly executed.

Cheering filled the halls of that magnificent campus, where each individual received the intense instruction needed to help Matthew conquer what is, for most, a simple skill. The entire faculty was responsible for Matthew's learning to walk. The next year he mastered holding a spoon so he could feed himself.

Several people thought this segregated campus, serving only individuals with special needs, should be closed, and all the students moved to the schools closest to their homes. While Jerry and I could appreciate other parents' opinions, we knew firsthand the benefits this type of setting provided Matthew, so we fought the efforts to close the school. The battle was ultimately lost, and the school closed after we moved away.

Surrounded

When Matthew was in fifth grade, and placed in a classroom with his typical peers for a good part of the day, it was often the other children who figured out what was best for Matthew. Open spaces became terrifying to Matthew at a young age. Unless he was in a pool, on a horse, in a wheelchair, or on his bike, he screamed. Not just a little scream, either; the blood-curdling type. He basically wanted to be attached to something, and moving, at all times.

Recess in fifth grade generally takes place outside. Matthew sat in a chair against the building, out of the sun and wind, and watched all the other children play. Until one day. Some students decided there had to be more to recess for Matthew than just sitting against a wall.

Several students formed a human circle. They got permission to get Matthew up and surrounded him, linking arms. Around the track they went. There were no blood-curdling screams, just encouraging words from a bunch of twelve-year-olds, and laughter from the middle of the circle.

Pearl S. Buck once said, "The test of a civilization is in the way that it cares for its helpless members."

Those kids passed the test.

When our family was transferred the following year, a young man from that class sent Matthew a letter:

Dear Matt Joyner,

I will miss you so much. When I first met you, I asked myself how can I be friends with someone that doesn't talk at all. But over the weeks and months I learned it doesn't take a conversation to have a friend.

The Beat Goes On

"We would like Matthew to be in band," a new high school teacher suggested, years later.

"And do what?" I was scared to ask.

"He loves music, and can hold onto a stick, so we were thinking about the snare drum," she cautiously went on. "What do you think?"

Matthew was cursed—and blessed, at the same time—with a mom who was extremely involved in his education and placement. After listening to the teacher's reasoning and research, I thought that maybe, just maybe, it could work. And, it did.

He was accompanied by one of his assistants, who sat with her hand on the stick. When it was Matthew's turn to play, she let go, and he hit the drum, and hit it, and hit it again, not wanting to stop. He was totally focused on the drum, knowing he could succeed in getting it to make a sound. She carefully reached over and gently held the stick until the director pointed at them again. It was the kind of classroom inclusion the parent of a handicapped child dreams of.

Shortly before the Christmas band concert, Matthew's knee became dislocated, leading to a long leg brace. As a result, we limited his walking to a minimum, and Matthew relied on his wheelchair to get around. I did not think it would pose a problem since Matthew was only participating in one song, and he could be wheeled on and off the stage quickly.

The band director, however, sounded panicky when he called. "We need Matthew standing for his number. Will he be able to do that? There is a special arrangement that will showcase his talents, and I need him out of his wheelchair."

Now, panic rose in me. "What special arrangement? Why does he have to stand to play the drum?"

I had flashbacks of so many meetings I had attended where we discussed appropriate inclusion. What did this man have in mind? I thought we had agreed the drum was working out fine, meeting goals on Matthew's Individual Education Plan (IEP) as well as proving to be something he enjoyed. In fact, he enjoyed it so much that Jerry and I had discussed buying Matthew a drum for Christmas.

"Trust me" was the answer I received. "Can he please just stand up for one number?" The band director sounded like he was on his knees on the other end.

"Fine."

Jingle All the Way

As instructed, Jerry and I had Matthew in his white dress shirt and tie. He sat in his wheelchair backstage. We sat on the front left row of the auditorium, not knowing what we would see or hear. His lead teacher had convinced us that quite a bit of thought and preparation by the team had gone into including Matthew in the program, and assured us we would not be disappointed.

As the band prepared for their fifth number, the director gave a recap of the semester and explained the second half of the program. Out of the corner of my eye, I spotted Matthew coming from behind the curtain. I nudged Jerry, and we sat in silence, watching a young man who was a foot taller than Matthew walk him onstage. He walked behind Matthew, holding him securely by the elbows, walking in perfect unison with our son's tin-man-like gait. How handsome they looked in their white shirts and ties.

Where is his drum? It was not onstage. *What now?* The boys stopped, faced forward, and I saw it. Hanging chimes. The young man stood behind the chimes, holding Matthew's hands. Matthew's eyes fixated on the chimes. Baton in air, the band director pointed in the direction of the chimes. One of Matthew's hands came up and gracefully brushed across the entire length of the chimes, creating the most beautiful sound.

The band played on, and every so often, at the most appropriate time, we heard the chimes. Of course, Jerry and I saw it too, since our eyes were on Matthew. It was a beautiful arrangement that showcased each instrument along with each student. What a gift.

The minute the piece ended, Matthew was escorted off the stage. One shining moment. One song. One perfect example of inclusion.

Involved in a Good Way

I found that teachers and parents of all children need to work together. One cannot be exclusive of the other. The poem "Unity," written by Cleo V. Swarat, was given to me the year I became president of the Parent-Teacher Association at Matthew's school. It was shared again a few years later when I served on the PTA at Drew's school. With the boys always attending different schools, I had twice the opportunity to serve, and be served.

The poem "Unity" describes beautifully the partnership that exists between a parent and a teacher for the benefit of the student. Some lines that spoke to me include, "Day after day the teacher toiled, with touch that was deft and sure; while the parent labored by his side, and polished and smoothed it o'er." It ends with, "For behind the parent stood the school, and behind the teacher the home."

The poem also points out, "And each agreed he would have failed if he had worked alone," a truth that applies to other aspects of life. I would have failed in raising Matthew had I not counted on his father—his earthly father as well as his heavenly Father—to help. When Jerry could not physically be there to help with Matthew's care or the problems that arose, the cheerleader in him came out, pushing and encouraging me to find solutions, giving me the confidence I needed.

The Chicken or the Egg

One of my first offensive plays with Matthew came with the insurance industry. Which came first? Had a diagnosis been made before or after our child was born? That became the million-dollar debate. In 1984, medical insurance companies had the right to disallow claims if they determined that an individual's health issues were preexisting.

"Your son's condition was diagnosed in utero, while you were pregnant with him. Therefore, we have placed all of his claims in the category of preexisting. He had all of these problems before he was born. Your son has no medical coverage." This was our insurance company's directive.

After hearing this verdict, I knew we would lose our house, cars, and everything else we owned as Matthew's medical bills mounted at an unfathomable rate.

Daily therapy could continue, I found out, even if I could only pay a small portion. I was told: *Just keep paying; whatever you do, don't skip a payment.* That way we would not lose anything. The hospitals, doctors, and therapists offered to write letters regarding Matthew's condition in an effort to have the decision reversed. I had the support of the medical community, which was comforting to an extent.

Still, a mailbox filled with dreaded bills at the end of each day dispelled any feelings of relief. I received duplicate and triplicate bills. It was a full-time job sorting, filing, and paying what I could.

Ironically, they told me that if I had elected not to have the amniocentesis that revealed his rare genetic abnormality, he would have had insurance coverage. The information we gained before Matthew was born carried the possibility of bankrupting us.

Jerry and I were going to have to go before a review committee. Fortunately, we never made it that far. Our claim was as rare as Matthew. There were no cases the insurance company could fall back on to seal their defense, so they had to give in. It felt like winning the Publisher's Clearing House Sweepstakes. Our mailbox was filled to overflowing with claims going back almost two years; all were now covered. Bills now read current because I had been paying at least twenty percent all along. Jerry continued to cheer me on.

Insurance Inadequacies

Many years later, my friend Meticulous Mary and I entered the conference room of one of the largest hospitals in Denver. At the table sat the CEO, the finance director, and the chairman of one of their larger clinics.

Matthew had a challenging year medically with numerous doctor, clinic, and hospital visits. The year had been filled with misbillings, misfilings, and ultimately calls from collection agencies, which led to my becoming a hysterical mess, a victim of circumstances. I needed to hire someone to help manage the mountains of paperwork that threatened to consume and bury me.

While venting on the phone one day to my dear friend Meticulous Mary, she volunteered to help, and came to my rescue. MM brought years of experience in the medical billing field, and that, combined with my intense desire to get on top of what I felt was a deteriorating insurance fiasco, we worked four days sorting, filing, matching Explanation of Benefit statements, preparing timelines, making copies, and typing notes.

MM and I decided the morning of the meeting, once everything was in order and laid out in neat stacks on the dining room table, that we needed something professional to carry our work in. Stopping by Jerry's office on the way into the city, we asked to borrow some of his leather portfolios to hold our neatly bundled packets.

"Whatever the outcome, ladies, you two sure look like winners," Jerry said with a big smile. Due to his workload, he did not have the time to help sort through and make sense out of our medical bills. He did, however, always have the time to speak encouragement.

The outcome of our meeting with the CEO, director, and chairman met and exceeded our expectations. The hospital wrote off entire bills for services that had not been filed in a timely manner. They combined duplicate accounts, resulting in reduced balances. We resubmitted several bills to the insurance company, which resulted in acceptance versus denials.

Our greatest satisfaction came a month later in a letter from the director of Patient Financial Services on behalf of the CEO, whereby they thanked MM and me for taking the time to meet with them and closed with, "It was an enlightening experience for all of us. I was very impressed with your preparation and documentation."

Matthew continued to unwrap the gifts God has given me.

5 In the Trenches

"A generous man will prosper; he who refreshes others will himself be refreshed." -Proverbs 11:25

Beautiful Bunch

The day Matthew was born, I received a gorgeous bouquet of yellow roses. My baby had been whisked away, along with my husband, to a larger hospital in Fort Worth. I was moved from the maternity floor to the general surgery floor so I would be out of earshot from crying newborn babies. The nurses thought our baby was going to die, so moving me was the kindest thing they could do.

My hospital room was quiet and stark. There were no calls or visitors at first—which I requested—only the yellow roses. They were enough for the time being as I lay waiting for the call informing me Matthew had passed away. I felt helpless and consumed with worry, and sleep evaded me.

The roses represented The Lunch Bunch, a group of neighborhood gals who were refreshing friends. The message on the card was simple: "Lifting you in prayer; call when you need us." To my surprise, none of them changed their phone numbers in the next year as I constantly reached out, asking for help.

The Prognosis

Though I was thankful to see Matthew alive the day he was born, I could not help wondering, *How long will he live?* While visiting me in the hospital two days later, Jerry informed me that the doctors wanted to operate on our sick baby boy.

"Operate on what? Why? He came out breathing on his own, Jerry, and you and I agreed that night we would not do anything heroic to save him. If he is meant to live it will not be because we intervene. Matthew has too many things wrong with him. We have to let him go. We cannot let him suffer anymore," I adamantly said to my husband, who looked like he had not slept for days; too busy traveling back and forth between two hospitals and home.

Jerry sorrowfully explained, "They say if we do nothing, we will cause a long and painful death. His kidneys are slowly shutting down due to all the damage the closed valve to his ureter caused. Fluid is backing up, and it is affecting his breathing."

Matthew had looked like a starving child—extremely skinny with a large, distended stomach—when I saw him for that instant before he was taken away.

"They want to detach his ureters and bring his bladder to the surface. He will have a little opening the size of a dime right below his belly button." Jerry continued to explain, repeating all the conversations that had taken place with the doctors.

"Why, Jerry? Why would we want to put Matthew through that?" Confusion and sadness filled my voice.

"Because, if we do not let them do this, they are saying we will cause a long and painful death," Jerry repeated. "This surgery will ease his discomfort. Like you say, Ann, he has too many things wrong with him. None of us is sure he is going to make it, but we need to make him more comfortable, like the doctors are suggesting."

Looking to each other for answers, we found none. What we did find was that our love for each other was somehow growing stronger in spite of the increasing emotional tension surrounding us.

Two days later I was able to hold Matthew for the first time, cherishing the moment, wondering if he would be alive tomorrow. He was hanging on. *He may not die after all.* Dr. Hometown and Reverend Kindness had been right.

Following the surgery, the doctors informed Jerry and me that Matthew would pee through the hole for roughly two to three years, until the time was right to go back in and do reconstructive surgery. The kidneys were badly damaged, and the ureters were shot. Time would hopefully heal them.

It Takes a Village

From the moment Matthew was born, we counted on our church community, The Lunch Bunch, relatives, friends, medical and educational communities, and, most importantly, God, to help with Miracle Man. Faced with raising a severely handicapped child at the same time we were, a friend wrote a poem, "Transformation," which spoke volumes to me, and she has given me permission to print it here:

> *When I saw the stone before me,*
> *I knew the choice was mine*
> *To take it up without regret*
> *Or leave it there behind.*
> *When I lifted it so freely,*
> *I saw that it was light.*
> *Not really stone at all*
> *But an angel taking flight.*

As we cared for our angel, the generous people who surrounded us also found themselves being transformed by Matthew.

A New Direction

Just short of Matthew's ninth birthday, Jerry accepted a job transfer.

Jeremiah 29:11 says, "For I know the plans I have

for you," declares the Lord, "plans to prosper you and not to harm you, plans to give you hope and a future." As we drove from Texas to Kansas City, this scripture rang out from the car radio on a Sunday morning in January.

I had been consumed by self-pity in the weeks and months prior to the move, knowing we were leaving behind the village we had so carefully constructed with the help of others, and my thoughts were anything but positive as we drove north. I felt abandoned and alone while driving with Matthew and Oprah, our beautiful black Labrador. Jerry and Drew were in the car ahead of us.

I tried unsuccessfully several times to find a radio station as we traveled through the Kansas plains. Besides the static from the radio, only an occasional bark or giggle from the backseat broke the silence that I filled with my sad thoughts.

The scripture unexpectedly cut through the quiet. "For I know the plans I have for you," declares the Lord, "plans to prosper you and not to harm you, plans to give you hope and a future." The reception could not have been clearer. I had picked up a signal from a Christian radio station.

Okay, God, I'm listening. You have my attention, especially since I seldom listen to Christian radio.

It was the message of hope I needed to hear. *How did you know, God?* I repeated that scripture over and over in the car that day.

We were on another journey, one we had not planned to take, and I heard the message that God would make it good.

Church in a Gym?

"Where are you going, Jerry?" I questioned as he took a right turn instead of going straight.

"You'll see," he said, smiling.

I was not in the mood for sightseeing in our new town. Leaving Drew to babysit Matthew without knowing anyone to call in an emergency made me extremely nervous, even though Drew was more than capable. I just wanted to try out the Methodist church in the established neighborhood I had found not too far from our house then get back to the kids.

Looking nervously at my watch, I angrily muttered, "Whatever you want me to see will have to wait. You are going to make us late for church."

Jerry triumphantly exclaimed, "We are on time!" as he pulled into a parking lot and found a parking space.

"On time for what?" I demanded. We sat in front of an elementary school.

"Ann, I read about this new Methodist church, and I think we should give it a try. They meet here in the school gymnasium."

"Seriously, Jerry? Church in a gym?" Looking at the school, I thought about the pretty little established church on the hill I thought we had agreed to try out. I was not happy. Chipper Jerry was, though; he was always ready to do something out of the ordinary. He opened my car door with a smile, encouraging me to join him.

Feeling like Dorothy in *Wizard of Oz*, I shook off my confused and dazed look after finding myself in a place I had been unwillingly deposited, knowing I could not sit in the car while Jerry went in to worship. Our church in Texas was pulling on my heartstrings; we had been so comfortable and settled just two weeks earlier.

When we walked through the front door of the school, a small crowd of happy people energetically greeted us. When we took our seats on cold folding chairs, I noticed the basketball nets, concrete walls, industrial floors, and a banner of the school mascot. Aside from the cross, the hymnals, and a few people wearing choir robes, it did not feel like a church. I crossed my arms and sat there thinking, *We will go to the church I want to next week.*

The Spirit and the Reverend

Jerry and I both felt it. The Spirit was present in that school gymnasium. We agreed on two things after worship: The young pastor was dynamic, relevant, and inspiring; the congregation was too small, too new, and not ready for a family like ours.

Instead of feeling excited about visiting other churches, I felt sad, knowing the one in the gym seemed perfect in so many ways. I reminded myself I had to trust that God had a plan, like the scripture said.

Jerry left town early the next morning on a business trip. I stayed at home with the kids, who were out of school for in-service, staring at boxes yet to be unpacked, with no friends to help, an impending snowstorm, and a homesick feeling for Texas. *How can life get any better in Kansas?* I wondered as I drifted off to sleep that night, praying for a new day and a new attitude.

I was always encouraged by a short piece called "Attitudes," written by Charles R. Swindoll, pastor and religious writer. In it, he writes, "The longer I live, the more I realize the impact of attitude on life… We cannot change the inevitable. The only thing we can do is play on the one string we have, and that is our attitude."

The blanket of snow that greeted me the next morning was breathtakingly beautiful, unlike the dreaded and treacherous snow-ice mix I was accustomed to seeing in Texas. With the snow came school closings, and having the boys home with me felt comforting. Drew was excited to hang out with Matthew and watch movies; he was in no hurry to acclimate to his new middle school. The snow had brought him a nice reprieve.

After receiving a call from one of The Lunch Bunch announcing a visit in a week or two, I found myself more content, concentrating on things I had to look forward to. Determined to make the most of being homebound for the day, I set my sights on getting the last of the boxes unpacked.

The doorbell interrupted my concentration. *Who in the world can that be?*

I looked through the peephole in the front door and immediately recognized the guy standing on my snow-covered porch: It was the pastor from the church in the gym.

What is he doing out in all this snow when everything in town is closed?

"Hi, I'm Pastor Adam," announced this man, looking even younger than I remembered. He held one hand outstretched to shake mine, and the other gripped a coffee mug and a card. "You're Ann, right? It's good to see you again. Do you mind if I come in?" he asked, kicking the snow off his boots.

"Why, of course not, please do," I hurriedly encouraged as the cold wind and snow tried to sneak past him. This man's Midwestern warmth immediately filled the house.

With a huge smile he explained, "I wanted to drop this coffee mug off to you and Jerry from the church and let you know how happy we were you chose to worship with us this past Sunday."

Looking at him I thought, *I hope this pastor cannot read my mind because, if he could, he would know I had intended on worshiping elsewhere.*

"We hope you plan to come back," he said as he strained to see who was in the living room. "And you have kids? Did they come as well? I'm sorry; it didn't mention kids in my notes," he said, appearing confused. As he hesitated, I took the opportunity to jump in.

"I really appreciate your stopping by, Pastor Adam. We can definitely use this mug because I have not found all of mine yet," I said, laughing, and pointed at some unopened boxes. "Yes, we do have kids, but we did not bring them to church with us. Jerry and I do not like to surprise people." I continued to explain as a questioning look spread across his face, "We have two sons. Our oldest is Drew, who is twelve, and Matthew just turned nine. He is our little miracle guy, who doctors said would not live. Mattie needs full assistance in almost everything because he is severely physically and mentally handicapped. He has never spoken a word." The puzzled look had disappeared from Pastor Adam's face, replaced by compassion and kindness.

"Well, I would like to meet them." He spotted the boys sitting in front of the TV and was drawn to them like a magnet. As he stepped onto the new carpet, I was glad most of the snow had melted off his boots onto the entry hall rug.

The boys became Pastor Adam's captive audience. After engaging in conversation with Drew for several minutes, he turned his attention to Matthew. Matthew sat in a small glider chair, rocking in a constant back-and-forth motion, his attention on the Disney movie instead of the stranger kneeling beside him.

After a minute or two of one-sided conversation, Drew said to Pastor Adam what I was thinking I had already shared: "Matthew does not talk."

Smiling, Pastor looked at Drew and gently said, "I know." He turned back to Matthew, continuing his conversation, all the while gently touching him. The Spirit I had felt in the gym now crept into my new living room.

After several minutes, the pastor came to where I stood, out of earshot of the kids. Apologetically I rattled off, "Pastor Adam, we really enjoyed your message on Sunday, everyone was very friendly, and everything we read about your new church sounds exciting, but Jerry and I feel that your church is probably too small. As you can see, our family is pretty high maintenance."

"Ann, I think you are wrong. God is doing amazing things in our congregation. I see Matthew as the beginning of a special ministry for children and families of children with disabilities at our church," he countered. "Would you be willing to give us a chance? Would you help us?" Adam pleaded with more excitement than a kid on Christmas morning.

"We just came from a large congregation in Texas where we created a program for Matthew. The participants had two large classrooms they came to each Sunday. Where would Matthew go?" I asked, trying to remember the space and layout of the school.

"I am not sure, Ann. What I am sure of is that I believe we are being called to be your church family. Can you give me a week or two to make a couple of phone calls?"

How could I possibly say no to this young, passionate pastor? *This could be part of God's plan,* I thought.

Angel Chris

The first call Pastor Adam made was to Angel Chris. Later, at a conference for Sunday school teachers, she shared her story of how she became involved in our lives:

> *Two years ago I returned home to find a
> message from my pastor on our answering
> machine. "Chris, this is Adam. A new family
> from Texas has joined our church. They
> have a severely physically and mentally
> handicapped son. I think he should be in your
> Sunday school class. They are very excited
> about this. Please give the Joyners a call. The
> mother's name is Ann; their son is Matthew."*
>
> *I listened to the message again. I could feel
> my heart beating faster. What was Adam
> thinking? My class was overcrowded as
> it was; there was a constant shortage of
> teachers! I had no degree in Special Ed! I*

have no degree in Special Ed for a reason.
don't feel comfortable in Special Ed classes.
Instead of calling Ann, I called Adam back. I
left a message with someone passing through
at the Activity Center. Adam did not call
back. I left another message. No return call.
It had been two days since Adam's message. I
had to call Ann Joyner back.

Have you ever met someone for the first time
and something just clicks? You immediately
start talking and laughing. You feel like
you have known them forever. This was my
feeling with Ann. Her smile, her warmth—
and, of course, that familiar Texas accent,
y'all! I loved her! She briefly explained
Matthew's disabilities and invited me to come
over to meet him the next day. I felt my heart
begin to beat faster again.

I prayed that night. Others I had talked to
about this had been fairly pessimistic: "This
will disrupt your class;" "No way;" "You are
definitely not qualified," etc.

So, I asked for help in dealing with Matthew.
I had no idea what to expect. What did he
look like? Act like? I thought back on my
unreturned calls from Adam, which had
forced me to call sweet Ann. There must be a
reason. Has your prayer ever been answered
before you were even finished praying? I think
mine was. I felt calm and at peace that night.
I was excited about this challenge and my
morning introduction to Matthew.

You notice his eyelashes first. Long, thick, and brown. Women would give anything for those lashes. Then you notice those big, brown, puppy-dog eyes. Matthew cannot talk, but he speaks with his eyes. I have seen happiness in those eyes; I've seen pain with tears, followed by strength and determination. As Matthew struggled through adolescence, I know I've seen a try-and-make-me *attitude. There is such gentleness about Matthew. He has hard, heavy braces on both legs and not a lot of control over where his arms may fly at any given moment, but there is a gracefulness about him. I think it is the grace of God surrounding Matthew.*

Matthew was a much-needed addition to my Sunday school class. During the fall, Ann came to class to explain to my third and fourth graders all about Matthew. They were encouraged to ask questions about him. My class was surprised to learn that Matthew loved swimming, and he could sign that he was thirsty by touching his lips.

Matthew's presence in my class helped teach us more about how Jesus wants us to live our lives than anything I could have found in a Sunday school curriculum guide.

I watched class bullies gently help Matthew stand up, and walk with him around our room with such care. Matthew brought out the kindness in them that I had not seen before—or even knew existed, based on some of their behavior in class.

*I had a mother call me about eighteen
months after her daughter and Matthew
had been in Sunday school together. The
daughter's gym teacher had called to thank
her for her daughter's kindness toward a
student with special needs. Evidently, only
a couple of students came forward to help,
and her daughter was one of them. The mom
felt the daughter might not have been so
willing to help if she had not enjoyed a class
with Matthew. I know God works through
Matthew.*

After Angel Chris finished speaking about a few other
experiences with Matthew, she looked over and saw one of the
Children's Education directors crying. That director shared
a story from her church that was the same situation exactly,
but they had turned the family away. The staff even voted
against trying to help this family and their son. This brought
about many concerns and comments from other members
in the class. One staff member had a similar story; many had
wondered what they would have done, and how their church
would have reacted. Their first comment was identical to
Angel Chris's first comment about me.

*"I have no Special Education degree! I have
no experience with Special Ed. I am not
prepared!"*

*Ann asked me if I could love and hug
Matthew like Jesus would. I said yes.*

"Then, you are prepared," she answered back.

*I thank God for Adam's phone call and
the Joyners' patience with my ignorance. I*

thank God for Matthew, with all his physical
complexities. He reinforces Jesus's simple
message: Love one another.

Answering the Call

Following Pastor Adam's and Angel Chris's first visits,
Vivacious Volunteer Coordinator (VVC) at the church went
into action. A notice appeared in the church newspaper
asking that anyone interested in meeting Matthew, a little
handicapped boy who had just moved to the area and needed
a church home, to please show up in the school cafeteria the
following Sunday morning.

There was no sign-up required; people were simply
encouraged to show up. While I got ready that morning, I
prayed for at least five people to show up. The church was
so small that possibly expecting five was too much; maybe
three would be nice. I grew more anxious by the minute, and,
although it was winter, I was sweating. Thank goodness the
kids' godmother (formerly known as GTB) had come for the
weekend to help. She was going to entertain Matthew at the
meeting, allowing me to give my full attention to the folks in
attendance.

She had forgotten to pack her dress shoes, however, which
only added to my apprehension as we all got ready to leave
the house. "No, Ann, I will not wear my tennis shoes. Just
give me a pair of your flats."

"You know my size tens will not fit, and they will look
ridiculous. Not to mention, you could break your neck," I
argued.

I should have known better than to argue. Godmother
got the shoes out of my closet herself. They turned out to be
the perfect fit for the situation, providing the comic relief we
needed as we walked into a meeting full of strangers.

At first I thought we had showed up at the wrong place in

the elementary school. *How many cafeterias can there be in this place?* There were sixteen people sitting on folding chairs in a circle. Surely they were not the folks who wanted to meet our Matthew? Obviously, I had underestimated how God was working in this new, small church. They were indeed the right group, smiling while watching Godmother gracefully shuffle across the room toward them, holding onto Matthew as he pushed his walker next to her. I followed closely behind, praying neither of them would fall.

Angels All Around

Our audience was as nervous as I in the beginning, but as they learned more about Matthew, their desire to help squashed any reservations they had. Everyone was drawn to the boy and the scripture from Matthew 25:40 (NRSV) that sat before them: "Truly, truly I say to you, just as you did it to the least of these, who are my family, you did it to me."

VVC rightly named the folks who volunteered to help with Mattie: Angel Care. Each Sunday one of our Angel Care team members greeted us at the front door of the school and escorted Matthew to the third- and fourth-grade Sunday school class, taught by Angel Chris. When Matthew became overwhelmed, his volunteer for the day took him to the library to play with some toys or just rested with him on a bench in the hall. No two angels looked alike. They were young, old, married, and single.

Pretty soon Matthew became a celebrity on campus. It seemed like everyone at this new little church wanted to get to know him, and us. We were surrounded by so many generous people, enabling us once again to be part of a faith community.

Matthew's volunteers began to thank us for allowing them to help care for him. God worked through our son, as some of his Angel Care workers shared:

Seeing the trust and love in Matthew's eyes and his joy in each accomplishment opens my eyes again to the wonders of life and God's love.

He taught me humility and gratitude.

You have brought us joy, and love, and fun, and more purpose, and have strengthened our faith.

All children are a blessing and a gift from God.

When Matthew reached up and touched my hand, I felt like Jesus had touched me.

On that snowy January morning, when Pastor Adam and I first met, he had a vision, and that vision became a reality. Matthew was joined by another little guy with special needs a few months later. And then, another. It was like the Field of Dreams: "If you build it, they will come." Matthew's Ministry was born in 1993.

The mission of Matthew's Ministry extends the love and message of Jesus Christ to all persons with special needs, and helps to incorporate them fully into the life of the church.

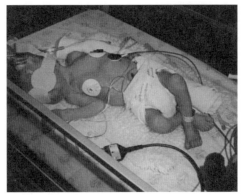

Matthew was hooked up to all kinds of tubes from Day 1.

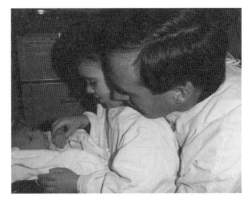

Drew meets his brother for the first time.

Matthew riding an adaptive tricycle while Drew
bikes alongside him.

Matthew with our new puppy, Oprah.

Family picture on Easter while visiting family in Houston.

Jerry catching Matthew after he came down the water slide with Drew at a local pool in the Kansas City area.

Matthew, Jerry, and Drew at Universal Studios in California.

Matthew, Jerry, and Drew in Durango, Colorado,
where Drew and Jerry kayaked.

Matthew and me in front of the JC
Nichols Fountain in Kansas City.

Drew and Matthew sharing a brotherly moment.

Matthew at age 16, shortly
after his cancer diagnosis.

Our family at Christmas one year.

6 Crying as an Aerobic Exercise

"Those who sow in tears will reap with songs of joy."

-Psalm 126:5

Hospitals

Someone once told me that the church is like a hospital, caring for broken and wounded people. I found myself needing the church, turning to God with increasing frequency, as Matthew spent time in hospitals. *Please, God, do not let this child suffer,* was my prayer from the beginning. That is why Jerry and I chose to let the doctors do his first surgery. They told us that if we did nothing, he would suffer significantly.

Reverend Cornelius J. Rempel, from the Mennonite Brethren Church in Canada, wrote:

> *What Suffering Is and Isn't: Nine Maxims to Ponder and Apply*
>
> *1. Suffering is not God's desire for us but occurs in the process of life.*
>
> *2. Suffering is not given in order to teach us something, but through it we learn.*
>
> *3. Suffering is not given to us to teach others something, but through it they may learn.*
>
> *4. Suffering is not given to punish us but is sometimes the natural consequence of sin or poor judgment.*

5. Suffering does not occur because our faith is weak, but through it our faith may be strengthened.

6. God does not depend on human suffering to achieve God's purposes, but through it God's purposes are sometimes achieved.

7. Suffering is not always to be avoided at all costs but is sometimes chosen.

8. Suffering can either destroy us or add meaning to life.

9. The will of God has more to do with how we respond to life, than with how life deals with us.

There were times Matthew was hospitalized when I was unable to hear, physically or mentally, the message a pastor or hospital chaplain tried to convey while I sat grieving over Mattie's prognosis. Often, once the choking sobs subsided and visitors departed, I found something left behind for me in the hospital room. One of those gifts, the paper with the maxims on suffering, serves as a reminder that God, along with us, did not want Matthew to suffer.

Coming Home

The day they told me Matthew would be released in a day or two from the hospital, Jerry arrived home from work to find me inconsolable. I had been crying for hours, thinking, *How in the world am I supposed to take care of my sick child? I have a secretarial degree, not a medical degree. They can barely keep him alive in the hospital. How will I be able to care for him at home?*

"Jerry, I do not want to bring him home. I am not ready. What if he dies here?" The pace and stress of traveling back and forth to the hospital each day, watching Mattie take two steps forward and three back, had taken a toll on all of us. Though having our family of four under one roof was something I had prayed for, the thought now filled me with terror.

My solid-as-a-rock, positive, upbeat husband assured me we would be fine, knowing some extra instruction on how to care for Matthew had been ordered. I spent the next two nights at the hospital learning more than I thought a layman, or should I say laymom, could.

"I need to do *what* with that thing?" I shivered at the thought. The sweet, overly patient nurse was holding a twelve-inch-long-by-one-third-inch smooth, round, steel rod.

"Gently insert it into the little hole in his tummy, here. Be careful not to go too far down," she warned as my eyes got bigger and my stomach somersaulted. "Here, you try." She carefully placed the instrument in my shaking, gloved hand.

After two days of practice, I was able to master the medical maneuver that prevented the little opening in Matthew's stomach closing. The other challenge we had to conquer was feeding. Our little guy could not suck very well. If the milk came out too fast, Mattie choked; if he had to work too hard to get the milk out, he wore himself out and slept. Every nipple ever invented was attached to bottle after bottle, until the nurses found one that would work for Matthew.

The first day a family brings a baby home from the hospital should be filled with joy. Our joy was mixed with apprehension. Matthew was taking us into uncharted territory. Many nights I lay in bed remembering the prayer I said before he was born: *Please do not give me Matthew if you are only going to take him away.*

Two and a half weeks later, Matthew was readmitted to the hospital. Failure to thrive was one of the characteristics of his chromosomal abnormality, which caused early death in previously reported cases. Our little guy was losing weight fast, so our assumption was that he was dying. We had been able to keep up with the prescribed feedings with one flowing right into the other sometimes, so the fact that we could now count his ribs was not making sense. It was heartbreaking to know that what we did was not enough. This was what I had so feared.

Following many tests, they discovered that Matthew's badly damaged kidneys were not producing, or holding onto, the amount of sodium his body needed. A quick, easy fix was put into place: A sodium cocktail was added to Matthew's formula. Six days later he was home again, looking more like his healthy, big brother had when he was a baby, chubby cheeks and all. The turnaround was amazing.

Miracle Man managed to stay out of the hospital for several months, and everyone around us marveled at how well our whole family was doing. Life was different than before Matthew, but it was not horrible. In fact, life was richer for Jerry, Drew, and me. We were finding out that each day was a gift, and taking nothing for granted.

What about Santa Claus?

The fact that Matthew lived to see his first Christmas gave us more reason to celebrate the season. Drew's best buddy, TBird, along with his two brothers, Godmother, and her husband, were coming for Christmas Eve dinner. Typical of kids getting sick around the holidays, Drew and Matthew had both come down with ear infections a few days earlier. But with antibiotics on board, I felt confident we could make it through Christmas without another visit to the doctor.

Matthew was especially out of sorts Christmas Eve day as I bounced back and forth between cooking, and feeding, changing, and rocking him. All the while, I wondered why the antibiotic was not kicking in. Finally, when the addition of baby Tylenol did not alter his spiraling-out-of-control cry, I thought, *Maybe a diaper change and the swing can calm him down. Jerry should be home any minute and can take over with Matthew while I finish cooking.*

When I removed the diaper, my heart stopped. Below Mattie's belly button and hole, on each side, two bulging masses appeared. Apparently, I screamed.

Drew appeared at the bedroom door with a scared look on his face. "Mommy, what's the matter?"

"Oh, bud, Mommy needs to get Mattie to the doctor. I think his ear is worse." I fought to remain calm.

"But you can't leave. Everyone is coming. It's Christmas Eve!" Drew argued, his little voice growing louder, his face looking anxious and confused.

"Don't worry, buddy. Mommy will hurry back," I lied, knowing in my heart that Mattie's first Christmas was not going to be at home.

I grabbed the phone and called Godmother to ask her to come to the house. I shouted instructions to her to take care of the half-prepared dinner, which included the turkey in the oven, watch Drew, and find Jerry. I loaded Matthew into his car seat and sped off to the doctors. I found that the pediatrician's office had just closed for the holiday when I called on the emergency line. "Get here as fast as you can," Dear Nurse said. "I will let the doctor know you're coming."

The pediatrician only took three minutes to diagnose bilateral hernias. Dear Nurse called the hospital when the examination was complete and told them to expect us. We were sent on our way.

I could barely see the road as I drove to Fort Worth. There were no storms outside, just internal ones that brought a flood of tears. *Why tonight, of all nights?*

Jerry was about a half hour behind me. Nurses grabbed a screaming Mattie from my arms at the emergency room entrance, leaving me to drown in a puddle of tears. What felt like an hour was fifteen minutes before a nurse came to get me.

As we walked back to where they had Matthew, she tried desperately to calm me; I had gotten more worked up by the minute. "Mrs. Joyner, he is going to be all right. I promise. We see hernias all the time, and this is something we can fix."

"I know Matthew will be all right. He, he, he al…ways is. He…is…a…fighter," I said, bawling, and trying to catch my breath. Louder than I thought, I said, "I have another child, you know. Who is going to be Santa Claus? He's supposed to come tonight. What am I supposed to tell Drew?" I was a momma out of control, shouting in the middle of a hospital corridor on Christmas Eve, filled with sadness for my two little boys.

"Excuse me," another nurse interrupted, while looking harshly at me and the nurse trying to console me. "Please keep your voices down. There are children here. Santa Claus will come," she stated, abruptly turning on her heels and heading down another hall.

At that point, my Santa rounded the corner. Jerry had finally arrived, and while the nurse filled him in, he held me, immediately recognizing that this was one of those times that was all he could do for me.

A few hours later they dismissed all three of us. Matthew had been given enough painkillers to make him look like he had a hangover. The crying had subsided, his little insides, which had been bulging, had been manipulated and pushed back in, and I swear he wore a grin. Our little fighter was ready to get back in the ring. We scheduled a surgery for two days after Christmas. All we needed to do was keep him from crying for seventy-two hours, and he would be fine.

Dinner was served at nine o'clock that Christmas Eve. The turkey was the best ever, having rested in the oven for more than six hours. We raised a glass with our friends, toasting Matthew's first Christmas. Drew laid out cookies and milk for

Santa Claus, and sure enough, he came that night. Both boys were happy and content on Christmas morning, home with their tired and relieved mommy and daddy. Joy replaced our tears once again.

And That Goes *Where?*

The surgery to close the opening in Matthew's stomach, repairing the bladder and reattaching the ureters, allowed us to retire the smooth, silver apparatus we had used to keep his little hole open. Always wondering what we could expect to encounter next with Matthew, Jerry questioned the surgeon at great length as to how the chromosomal abnormality would play out. There were many characteristics of Ring 22 that we had yet to see manifest in Matthew's first two years.

The doctor's response was so matter of fact; there was no opportunity for further questioning. "I have no doubt that someday we will have this genetic mishap figured out, but not in my lifetime." The doctor was Jerry's age.

Matthew peed like a regular little guy after the surgery. But, not for long. Urine backed up again, causing more damage to his kidneys. Catheterization was the answer, until his plumbing could readjust to performing on its own.

Once I got the knack of inserting the little red catheter into his little penis, we managed to keep him draining. Six to eight times a day, I'd change a diaper that was a tiny bit wet, and follow that up with getting the rest of his urine out. Although this went on for years, I can count on one hand how many times Jerry performed this procedure!

Jerry was the one who gave almost every bath, and smoothed lotion over every inch of Matthew's body. He also was in charge of Mattie's nails, shaving, and haircuts. There was just something about the little red catheter that Jerry could not handle.

The Longest Stay

Like a scrawny, lightweight prizefighter who would not give up, Miracle Man fought his way through several more surgeries. Often we wondered, *How much more can this little guy take?* Other times Jerry and I wondered, *How much more can we take?*

St. Francis de Sales, a bishop of Geneva who was honored as a saint in the Roman Catholic Church, said: "Do not look forward to what might happen tomorrow. The same everlasting Father who cares for you today will take care of you tomorrow and every day. Either he will shield you from suffering, or he will give you unfailing strength to bear it. Be at peace then and put aside all anxious thoughts and imaginations."

By the time Matthew was ten years old, his scoliosis (curvature of the spine) had worsened to the point that it affected his breathing and ability to walk. First and foremost in each and every decision Jerry and I made for Matthew, we focused on the quality of his life, not necessarily extending his life. We strived to make each and every day a good one, knowing it might be the last.

We faced a tough choice with Matthew's scoliosis. We could do nothing, which would soon have him back in a wheelchair, without the ability to walk (with his lungs and other organs being compromised as well). Or, we could choose to have his back fused with rods that stabilized his spine. Walking was one of the things that brought Matthew great joy. He was making up for lost time, since he took his first independent steps when he was seven. Knowing how much he loved to walk, we chose the surgery.

Matthew went through ten hours of surgery, a week in the intensive care unit, two weeks on the general surgery floor, four days home, then back in intensive care for another week with a collapsed lung.

When asked, "How do you do this?" our answer was

always the same:

"Our faith. Tested each time? Definitely. Strengthened even more? Absolutely."

Weeks ahead of the surgery, our church family, neighbors, relatives, Matthew's teachers and therapists—everyone we knew—concocted their own little plan to help carry us through. From a surgery waiting room filled with praying people who fed us, consoled us as we received each update, and encouraged us, to people who cooked, ran errands, cared for Drew, or stayed at the hospital for hours on end with Jerry or me, everyone involved played an integral part in Mattie's recovery.

Notes were left in "Matthew's Visitors' Book," which I read to him each night as he tried to sleep. Ones like the following, combined with IV medications, cut through our son's pain, as well as our own:

> *Dear Matthew,*
>
> *You're resting now after a really rough night. Angel Chris, VVC, and your mom are sitting around the room. We're getting ready to pray for you, asking God to strengthen you. His angels have stood by your bed each night. You are precious to God, and your life has shaped so many others. I know Jesus loves you with a very special love. I am praying for you every day.*
>
> *Love, Pastor Adam*

Where There Is Music

Cellulitis was the diagnosis several years later. Matthew woke up one day with his arm, the one that had the cancer, bright red and swollen like a balloon. At first, we were convinced it was the rare, deadly form of cancer returning and rearing its ugly head, but instead found that it was an awful infection of connective tissue that just happened to be in his same weak arm. Hospitalization, with massive doses of high-powered, antibiotics via IV, was ordered.

Diversion was the key to keeping Matthew content in hospitals, to keep him from crying or trying to rip his IVs out. Getting an IV in was awful for him, requiring a skilled phlebotomist and my holding him still with every ounce of strength I had. Even the most tenured phlebotomist was sometimes unsuccessful, and I had a strict "you have two tries" rule, so there was always another tech close by. Matthew had long abandoned his coping mechanism of laughing at a shot or needles. After so many, he figured out what was coming. As traumatic as it always was, Matthew always forgot the discomfort we put him through, his smile and sweet laugh returning, with simple diversions.

It was an unexplainable blessing that so many of his hospitalizations occurred during March Madness. Mattie's love of basketball had been nurtured early on by Drew. When a game was on, little else mattered, in either of their worlds. This time, though, Matthew felt pretty rotten, and the infection in his body seemed to be getting worse.

The singing bunny brought peals of laughter, though, another diversion Miss Knowing bought him. She knew the right time to come to our rescue in the hospital, and more importantly, knew when to call in extra troops. However, a few days into our stay, basketball, singing bunnies, Drew and his buddies, and other visitors, could not help Matthew turn the corner this time.

And so, Miss Knowing, well aware that Matthew loved music, especially the praise choir at church, pulled out all the stops. That day, when nothing else worked, five wonderful members of the choir showed up in Mattie's hospital room. Miss Knowing knew that was better than any medicine the doctors could have ordered, and she somehow made it happen.

Matthew, upon seeing the choir, became overly excited with his uncoordinated clapping and rocking. After trying to restrain him a few times, because his IV almost came out, we decided his pure bliss—even just fifteen minutes' worth—was worth the risk. The nurses managed to make a wonderful splint that held everything in place with surgical tape. We let him rock and roll with the group.

Later that evening, I had the best night's sleep ever in the hospital on the hard, cold, plastic-chair-turned-into-a-bed, as did Mattie. The songs of praise had filled our hearts and heads, as well as the hallway, inviting the Spirit to soar through our hospital wing.

Guilt Is a Four-Letter Word

Parents need a break. That includes parents of handicapped children. Many of my friends said, "But I feel guilty leaving Johnnie or Suzie."

My reply every time was, "Feeling guilty is a waste of time and energy." Jerry and I were better able to take care of Mattie when we took care of ourselves. Sometimes that meant a vacation for just the two of us; other times we would took Drew and left Mattie behind. Then there were occasions when Jerry shipped me off alone to be with relatives or friends. He had a sixth sense of when those trips were needed. I was always a better momma, and wife, after a break.

Sometimes we were really adventuresome and let ourselves be talked into vacationing at a friend's house. Jerry's fraternity brothers organized a reunion of four families when the kids were two and five, and taking a flight versus driving made the most sense.

The four of us looked like the von Trapp family from *The Sound of Music* as we boarded the plane, following Drew as he excitedly skipped to our row of seats. Khaki pants for all three guys, and me in my new, homemade, plaid cotton skirt. Outfits had been carefully coordinated because I wanted us to all look our best when we got to the reunion. Drew climbed into the window seat, with me in the middle, Jerry on the aisle, and Matthew sharing Jerry's and my laps. Everything was stowed away as we prepared for takeoff.

Shortly after takeoff, Matthew got the giggles. He started laughing louder and louder. Folks around us thought he was pretty cute, including the flight attendants who came by to serve us drinks. Snacks and drinks filled Drew's and my trays, while Mattie filled Jerry's lap, in more ways than one.

When Jerry shifted our little guy from one leg to the other, we looked down to see a large wet stain on Jerry's thigh. Being wet was one thing, but suddenly, an all too familiar smell hit the cabin. Then we discovered Matthew had pooped, with some leaking out of his diaper, through his cute little outfit, and onto Jerry.

Mortified, I moved everything to Drew's tray so I could get the diaper bag. Of course, it was huge, due to the amount of paraphernalia we had to keep with us at all times, making it all the more difficult to dislodge from under the seat in front. I fished out a diaper, a new outfit, and wipes. Looking back toward the bathroom, I noticed the refreshment cart blocking our way, so I had no choice but to go forward to the bathroom in first class. Turbulence hit just as I exited our row.

"The drinks are spilling. I need help," Drew pleaded.

"Not now, Drew," Jerry yelled. "You'll just have to handle it. Matthew has had an accident." He was frustrated as he looked down at his pants. Drew looked like he was going to burst into tears.

Looking at Jerry, I yelled back through gritted teeth, "Do not yell at him. This is not his fault," and I threw a handful of wipes at him as I climbed into the aisle, Mattie over one arm, my supplies cradled in the other.

Upon entering the bathroom, I looked at the tiny space. I

set Matthew on the sink to try to figure things out, apparently hitting the faucet and turning on the water. To further complicate our predicament, more of Mattie's accident ran down his leg, and the smell was worse. *If this plane hits one more bump, I swear I am going to throw up,* I thought. Finally, I figured it out.

Putting the lid down on the toilet and hiking my skirt up, I sat down, placing Mattie on the floor, his head touching the door and his legs up in the air. As quickly as I could, between the bumps, I managed to strip him down totally and, using all the wipes and paper towels available, almost had the job complete. The door opened.

"Oh. Excuse me," the surprised copilot shouted, slamming the door. Unfortunately with the door opening, Matthew moved a little, which now caused the door to hit his head and make him cry. Add to that, another bump, another wave of nausea. *Never again,* I thought.

Jerry and Drew had both recovered by the time I got back to the seat. Everything was in order, and they were talking and looking out the window. "Mattie looks good," Jerry said, smiling as I handed him off. "Where is his other outfit?"

"It belongs to the airlines now, Jerry. I forgot to take a bag to bring it back. Lesson learned. Another lesson learned: Always lock the bathroom door." I laughed as I shared the entire story, trying to smooth out my wrinkled new skirt.

We exited the plane looking like the von Trapp family undone. Jerry's fraternity brother first asked him about his pants. He looked pretty bad, not to mention smelling like one big baby wipe. Our friends knew our challenges and loved us all the more for making the effort. We learned on that trip, and every other we took, that once we made it to a destination, friends and family would take over caring for Mattie, and my *never again* thoughts were replaced with, *Where to next?* Grammy's and Jerry's siblings' houses, as well as Godparents' lakehouse, were frequent getaway destinations with the kids.

Angels in Disguise

Who would have thought that one of our most beloved sitters would be a young man whose parents often were ready to strangle him? Gentle Giant had a way with both boys, which was a gift we all cherished. When it was nice outside, GG would have Matthew strapped on his three-wheel, specially designed bike, pushing him around the driveway, while shooting hoops with Drew at the same time. Neither of the boys seemed happy to see Jerry and me return home after they'd spent time with Gentle Giant.

Years later, upon applying for college, GG wrote about "Respect for Others," addressing the following statement presented:

> *No two people are alike. A vital self-esteem builder is to admire, respect, and appreciate the uniqueness of other people. Recognizing the differences in others will provide you with your own special place of importance in this world and strengthen your own self-esteem.*

His response, printed verbatim with permission:

> *The qualities I look for in people are those of strength through adversity. Oddly enough, the one person for whom has been my resource of more inspiration and respect is a person who is very close to me but for whom I have never had a conversation. This very special person is a little boy who was born ten years ago with a rare genetic abnormality. 'Strength Through Adversity' is the only phrase that comes close to describing the immense spirit of this boy and his relentless family. Matthew has gone from a birth defected fetus to the*

walking, laughing, smiling, and most of all,
loving human that he is today. Matthew's
story is worthy of ten times more respect he
and his family will ever receive, from me or
anyone else.

Matthew inspired numerous sitters throughout his journey. We found, as GG said, "No two people are alike." Good things come in small packages. Two little boys and a girl moved next door to us just about the time Drew became of age to babysit. The Trio adored their newfound sitter and his different little brother, and oftentimes the five of them were together when Jerry and I went out on a date with the Trio's parents. As it turned out, the Trio grew up, and, although younger than Mattie, became his sitters, often with the help of Tiny but Mighty, their mom. TBM made Galatians 6:10 come alive for her Trio: "Therefore, as we have opportunity, let us do good to all people." Whenever they had the opportunity to help us with Matthew, they did.

So did Angel Man. He appeared in our lives when we moved to Kansas City. As we stood in front of our new congregation one day, he approached our family and said, "If you all ever need a break, I would love to come watch Matthew."

Who sent you? I stood looking at Angel Man in total shock, knowing exactly *who* had sent him. Honestly, with just moving to a new city, Jerry and I wondered if we would have another date before Drew was old enough to watch Matthew.

Besides friends, there were teachers, para-professionals, and therapists we hired for a night out, or a weekend away. Each and every one of these people was an angel. They chose to be with our son, and helped us grow into better parents.

Jerry and I were continually amazed at the effect Matthew had on people. God works through people—sometimes the people you would least expect, like Mattie—to accomplish his purposes.

7 Gracious Receiving— and Giving

"God has given us two hands—one to receive and the other to give. We are not cisterns made for hoarding; we are channels made for sharing."
-Billy Graham

Seeing and Believing

The church bulletin announcement jumped out at Jerry and me, asking for volunteers to assist with a special needs Boy Scout troop. Although the troop was supported financially by our church family, it lacked the hands-on support needed to make sure each participant experienced success. After Matthew came to our lives, our eyes became open to new and rewarding opportunities. We felt called to participate.

I will never forget one of the first nights I volunteered with these young men. It was the night they worked on earning their knot-tying badge. The only knot I knew how to tie was the one on Drew's shoes. *What in the world was I thinking when I volunteered for this?* I wondered. Better yet, what was God thinking when he nudged Jerry and me to step forward to help these individuals? There is a huge difference in dealing with babies with special needs versus young adults.

I felt more frustrated as the evening went on, but the fear of failing these young men kicked my determination into gear. I found the book with step-by-step instructions and led them through a successful knot-tying session. At the end of the evening, the scouts looked like they had reached the top of Mt. Everest, exuding pure joy.

Rose Fitzgerald Kennedy once said, "Life isn't a matter of milestones but of moments." I saw that in these young men. And I began to see it in Matthew. This volunteer opportunity encouraged me to find joy in our Mattie's small triumphs instead of feeling disappointed in his lack of accomplishments. I threw away the book I had followed so faithfully with Drew, the one that tells moms at what age their babies should be doing what.

Crawling on his tummy was a huge triumph for Matthew. For several years he scooted around on his back, pushing off with his feet. Jerry's sister claimed her wood floors had never been as shiny as they were after Matthew spent a few days scooting around her house while we vacationed with Drew. When he finally started crawling on his tummy, we noticed it: The crooked spine was becoming worse.

Free?

We added to our growing number of hospitals and specialties, Texas Scottish Rite Hospital for Children (TSRHC) in Dallas. To become a patient of TSRHC, one must have an orthopedic condition and be referred by a physician. Recalling the preexisting condition nightmare we experienced with insurance when Matthew was born, Jerry and I obviously felt anxious about what lay ahead. We had been told Matthew's scoliosis was progressing rapidly, and they were the experts in that field, so we set up the appointment, knowing we wanted the best care available. We would face the insurance issue when the time came.

After Mattie's initial exam from head to toe, where meticulous measurements of his spine were recorded from a myriad of X-rays, we stopped by the pharmacy to pick up a prescription that would hopefully help the minor seizures he was having. Up to that point, we had been treated like royalty, so I was taken aback when the gal handing over the medicine looked at the checkbook I pulled out and barked, "Put that away." No explanation.

Leaving, I thought possibly we had met our deductible

and it was covered 100%. The following day, I received a call from the hospital wanting to make a three-month follow-up appointment for more X-rays. When I asked the scheduler about billing, she informed me that someone else would give me a call.

Matthew's referral to the orthopedic clinic allowed him to be seen by all the other clinics as well. It was a month after our first visit, when Matthew was being admitted for dental surgery at Scottish Rite, that we found out exactly what we were receiving. The hospital took no payments from patients, and—because Matthew was being seen there for his scoliosis—he could also be seen for his other medical needs. We discovered that TSRHC is not a United Way agency and does not receive state or federal funding. Instead, the hospital relies on the generosity of individuals, organizations, foundations, and corporations to continue its mission. What a tremendous gift we were given.

After spending two nights in TSRHC following oral surgery, Matthew received another free gift. Music Man, our church choir director, thought a black Labrador retriever would be good medicine for Matthew. We sat around a few days later with MM, his wife, and two other precious friends, and unanimously agreed to name our new, gorgeous puppy Oprah. In a house full of boys, you would think I would have been overjoyed to have some female companionship. Instead, she provided me with more challenges, which I really did not need. *What were our friends thinking?* Everyone was happy but Momma.

Manna from Heaven

Thankfully, Oprah was the most extravagant present our family received after one of Matthew's hospitalizations. The outpouring of gifts always included meals—nourishment for both body and soul—which were hard to accept in the beginning. We found ourselves transformed from an independent young family of three, to a family of four who were totally dependent on other family, neighbors, and the church, to meet even our basic needs.

When I expressed concern to Jerry over receiving so much, his reply was, "Don't worry, Ann. Our turn will come when we can help someone else." He was young but wise. So we began to practice gracious receiving. Once we conquered that skill, we embraced more and more the opportunities to give back.

Cooking always brought me joy, and I found it to be great therapy. It took my mind off of dwelling on our problems, and forced me to focus more on helping others. I often say, "Cooking is therapy, and some weeks I need more than others." It really was a terrific outlet for me, especially after a few disastrous attempts at joining support groups for parents of children with special needs. I walked out of the meetings sometimes thinking, *I guess I should be sadder than I am.* Then I remembered I had a choice, and my choice was to head to the kitchen, which brought me joy.

"The Happy Cooker," a nickname I picked up along the way, stuck. At one point I turned my cooking into a little business, able to work from home, which was perfect with Matthew. When approached for donations, I was nervous and excited at the same time. *Can my therapy actually raise money for a good cause?*

Dinners in the Freezer was a favorite package I chose to donate to church auctions, usually held to raise money for missions. There was always someone in need of ten to twenty frozen dinners. Appealing-sounding menus, filled with comfort food, would have several attenders bidding on my donation. It was humbling and nerve-racking at the same time, especially when I saw a new church employee bidding against the senior pastor. The new employee was not intimidated in the least by the other bidders, and was successful in getting the item for his pregnant wife and two boys. He knew it would come in handy.

The auctioneer asked if I would perhaps offer it to the second-highest bidder. That same evening a woman bought it for her aging parents. When I delivered the dinners to people's homes, the gracious recipients thanked me more times than I could keep track of. What people failed to realize was how much this meant to Jerry and me; we were given the chance to give back a portion of what had been given to us. And so was Matthew. God was multiplying all of our gifts.

Matthew's Turn

Matthew could not speak or write, so often his communication came through me because I knew exactly what he was thinking. We wrote the following letter to Pastor Adam:

> *Of all the gifts I have to give, I never thought money would be one of them. When I turned eighteen this past January, I became eligible to collect SSI (Supplemental Security Income) from the government due to being permanently disabled and unable to work.*
>
> *I have my own money now—yeah! I got my first check last Friday.*
>
> *I am glad you are still totaling the gifts for the God's Plans, Our Hands capital campaign, because I would like mine to be counted in. Here is my commitment card for a $1,000 total gift over the next three years.*
>
> *God has done amazing things with my life, and I know we are smiling together with this opportunity I am able to be a part of.*
>
> *My Love, in him, forever and ever,*
> *Matthew*

In Luke 6:38 it says, "Give, and it will be given to you." Matthew witnessed this over and over again.

At Thanksgiving one year, our family served dinner at City Union Mission in downtown Kansas City. Drew loaded up food plates in the kitchen, Jerry delivered them, I filled water glasses, and Matthew sat in his wheelchair by the piano, rocking back and forth, enjoying the holiday music. *This is the perfect serving opportunity for our whole family,* I thought as I went to the back to refill the water pitchers.

When I returned to the dining hall, panic consumed me. Where was Matthew? At the piano, all I could see was that a group of men had gathered. Mattie was nowhere. I rapidly made my way to where I had left him, and spotted one of Matthew's wheelchair wheels next to a gentleman leaning over and clapping in the same, uncoordinated way Matthew did. The two of them clapped in unison, with several other homeless gentlemen around, all having a wonderful time.

My worried look interrupted the fun. Seeing that all was well with Mattie, I quickly explained, "Oh, there he is. Sorry, I just lost sight of him for a minute. He is handicapped and cannot talk." They all looked at me like I was from outer space.

"We know that," said the man who had been clapping in unison with him. "So? He is just like us. You know what? Most of society looks at him just like they look at and think of us," he said, rubbing Mattie's shoulder, as another song and more rocking began. They turned their backs to me, leaving me to unravel my thoughts.

Later, when we left, several men thanked us for bringing Mattie, and we thanked them for allowing him to be part of their Thanksgiving celebration. Everyone agreed that God, who values each and every human being, had blessed us all with gifts we can share.

Watching the interactions between Mattie and some of his

friends with special needs taught me more about how to treat people than I could have learned anywhere else. All people want is love, attention, and a feeling of acceptance. They crave that. We all do. It is essential to our well-being.

When Matthew was a teenager and met Miss Barbie Doll, a teenage gal with Down syndrome, fireworks lit the sky. There was magic between them. The two never quit laughing or smiling in each other's presence. It was the ideal relationship: MBD talked Matthew's head off. She was just fine with the fact that he did not talk. In fact, it was probably better that he couldn't. She felt secure with Matthew in the knowledge that she was able to help someone with a lesser ability, and their relationship filled her with a confidence she had yet to experience with other friends. She showered him with movies on special occasions, and he showered her with Barbie dolls. The most precious gift they gave each other, though, was their unconditional love. That is what I witnessed, too, between Matthew and the homeless men.

Called to Teach

Jerry possesses the gift of teaching. After his stint with sixth graders and occasionally substitute teaching in an adult Sunday school class in Texas, he was encouraged to lead a Sunday school class for adults at the little church that met in the gym in Kansas. It was only a few months after we joined the church, with a team of five people taking care of Matthew each week while we worshiped, when Jerry was called.

"Jerry. You cannot commit to that," I argued. "That would mean they have to come up with more folks to take care of Matthew. We have five now, one for each Sunday. No one is going to commit to watching him three hours each Sunday."

"Well, Pastor Adam asked me, Ann. So, do you think you could go to VVC and see what she can do?" Jerry really wanted to do this, but I felt like we were already over taxing this new little church with our high-maintenance family.

I was wrong. Within two more weeks, VVC had another team in place to care for Mattie during the second hour. That meant our family could worship together while he was in Sunday school with Angel Chris and a helper. After that, there was another angel who watched him while Jerry became instrumental in starting Morning Star, a new class for adults. The more we were given, the more we were able to give back.

Sometimes there was only Jerry, myself, and one or two other people in the Morning Star class. It was almost impossible to grow and invite people to join us when we met in a hallway located outside the nursery, sometimes having to help rock babies during class time. It was difficult to see where this class would end up.

It ended up in our house. Yes. Every Sunday for almost a year, the class met in our home, due to the fact that the church was out of room and we had no other place to meet. Our house was close to the church, and it appeared to be the perfect solution.

Sunday mornings were a hoot during that time. Ladies showed up early to start the coffee and lay out breakfast items, Jerry and some of the other men rearranged the furniture so everyone could fit, and I flew around, finishing dressing Matthew and myself. There were times I wondered why we had volunteered for such a crazy endeavor, especially after we sometimes entertained other friends on Saturday evenings and stayed up way too late.

Then, I saw what was happening. The class grew and grew and grew. One day I came out of Matthew's room and saw the living room overflowing with people. They lined the steps going to the second floor. Also, there was Jerry, leading the group in a lesson he had spent hours preparing. Everyone grew in their faith. The Spirit—the one I knew was present in that same living room the day Pastor Adam came to visit when we first moved in—was also there each and every Sunday.

Called to Serve

Do all the good you can,
By all the means you can,
In all the ways you can,
In all the places you can,
At all the times you can,
To all the people you can,
As long as ever you can.

This quote, by the founder of Methodism, John Wesley, was a framed reminder in our house that we are all called to serve.

Mentor Man, the youth pastor, was a huge part of Drew's life, encouraging him to join in on mission trips. Drew's travels to Alabama, Texas, Colorado, West Virginia, and Illinois gave him the opportunity on several occasions to share his gifts with other people who were less fortunate than he. I cherished seeing the pictures, which spoke thousands of words, at the conclusion of each trip.

When Drew graduated high school, one of the gifts Jerry and I gave him was a video montage from the day he was born until the day he graduated. Carefully selected songs accompanied each group of pictures. Eric Clapton's "Change The World" plays while Drew is seen with kids on his shoulders, shooting hoops, playing in the sand, teaching Vacation Bible School, and just hanging out with kids.

The smiles on the children's faces, as well as Drew's, were right in line with the chorus of Clapton's song: "That I can change the world. I would be the sunlight in your universe." Drew was definitely their sunlight in the short time he had with each of them. He changed their worlds, making them a little better, if only for brief moments.

He was also Matthew's sunlight, especially when they were both teenagers and able to visit their godparents' lake house.

Getting Matthew on and off the pontoon boat took careful planning and execution. The house sat high on a hill, and it was impossible to access the boat with Mattie from their property.

There was another dock a few doors down, though, and with everyone's determination, we all got on the boat, wheelchair and all. Most often, Mattie felt secure sitting in his chair as the boat gently drifted across the water. Every once in a while, Drew put his brother in the captain's seat, with his hands on the wheel, and he drove the boat just like any other teenager. "That I can change the world. I would be the sunlight in your universe."

8 The Power of Brotherly Love

*"Whatever you did for one of the least
of these brothers of mine, you did for
me." -Matthew 25:40*

In the Beginning

Even before Matthew was born, an extraordinary relationship existed between him and his three-year-old brother, Drew. Realizing our baby could be stillborn, Jerry and I chose the name Matthew knowing it meant "gift from God." He was conceived in love, and however long God lent him to us, Matthew was our gift.

Drew was ecstatic when we broke the news months earlier that he would be a brother. He patted my tummy every time he was near, and talked to his baby brother. As the weeks dragged by, I wondered when and how I would tell him his brother may die, knowing how painful it would be.

One afternoon, shortly before Christmas, Drew crawled up on my lap while I sat in our overstuffed recliner. Drew nestled in; my chin rested on his head; he began to knock softly on my tummy. "Mat-hue! You in dare? How ya doin'?"

Looking beyond him to the door that led to our backyard, I had the urge to run through it so I would not have to tell my sweet Drew the terrible news about Matthew. However, I knew the time was right to prepare him.

My throat started to close as I groped for the right words. Nothing in the cute little books we read about becoming a big brother had prepared me for this.

How in the world would Drew, a carefree little boy, handle the news that his brother might die? Would he be uncontrollably distraught, a thousand times more than when his goldfish had died? Would he be angry, and stay that way?

Would he ever trust me again? First, I had told him he would be a big brother, and then to tell him that might not happen? Would he think I was dying also? Questions swirled in my head, making me feel dizzy and nauseated.

The Crushing Blow

I swallowed my fear and gently explained, "Baby Matthew is very sick."

Drew looked up, puzzled. "Sick? How do ya know he's sick?"

Looking into his big, brown, questioning eyes, I fought back the tears by biting the inside of my cheek. "He doesn't move around inside Mommy's tummy or kick like he is supposed to."

"Oh. Did I kick a lot when I was in dare?" Drew asked, pointing to my stomach.

"Yes, you kicked *all* the time." I paused, watching the grin spread across his face, his eyes sparkling, wishing I didn't have to continue. "The doctors told Daddy and me he will probably die."

Immediately the sparkle went out of Drew's eyes. Was I seeing fear, sadness, or…what? My heart broke, realizing I could not make things better for either of my children.

Drew pulled back his hand from where he had been patting Matthew, formed it into a little fist, and punched me in the stomach, screaming, "No! He won't die!" and slid off my lap. His big, brown eyes glazed over as he looked at me pleadingly, as if to say, "Mine! Dat's my brudder in dare, and I'm gonna have him. You said I could. You said I would!"

Before I could react, Drew hightailed it out the same door I had so badly wanted to run out just a few minutes earlier. Matthew, on the other hand, reacted.

I felt the faintest kick, which took me by surprise. I could not remember the last time I had felt movement. Wasn't it during the amniocentesis? Was this another sign?

First Glimpse

The first time Drew saw Matthew was in an intensive care unit in the hospital. This was a step-up unit from the critical care room where Matthew spent his first week.

After Jerry scrubbed Drew's hands, arms, and face at the sink located just inside the intensive care unit, a nurse helped him into a gown. The sterilized coverings were one-size-fits-all. "All" did not include little boys. With the gown wrapped, tied, and securely fastened around his body, Drew held up his hands, looking like a miniature doctor ready to perform surgery. We all laughed, which helped ease the tension that had mounted in the room. He was ready to meet his brother.

A few minutes earlier, one of the nurses had transferred Matthew from the intimidating bed, where he spent most of the day, to my arms. The monitors, lights, cords, and bags filled with fluid all disappeared when I saw Drew with his bright eyes approach Matthew and me.

When did Drew grow from a toddler into a little boy? He suddenly appeared much bigger and older to me.

"Hi Mat-hue. It's me, Drew, your big brudder," he announced as his face lit up like a Christmas tree.

I sat in the rocking chair, cradling Matthew, careful not to disturb any of the wires that monitored his breathing, heart rate, and IV fluids. I glanced back and forth from fragile Matthew to his precious older brother and held my breath.

I prayed that no bells or alarms would go off while he inspected Matthew. I did not want Drew to be afraid of his brother. Drew touched Matthew's face, his hands, and started to undo the blanket to see what was underneath.

"Careful, buddy," Jerry said.

Drew turned, never releasing Matthew's hand, and looked at his daddy, who hovered protectively. Jerry snapped a picture, and another, then another.

When the pictures were developed a week later, I clearly saw the look on Drew's face that said, *I told y'all he wasn't gonna die!* He beamed, so proud of his little brother, who continued to fight to stay alive.

Matthew came home ten days later, looking sick and pale. Drew stayed close as I cared for Matthew. He stroked Matthew's cheek, patted him on the head, and talked to him while I spent hour after hour trying to get Matthew to eat.

Jesus said, "Whatever you did for one of the least of these brothers of mine, you did for me" (Matthew 25:40). Drew brought this scripture to life for me as I watched him minister to his frail and broken brother.

A Christmas Story

Jerry and I learned to stand back and let Drew take the reins when it came to hanging out with his little brother. Little did we know, he would one day literally hold the reins *on* Matthew.

Drew loved to act. He presented plays, especially around the holidays. The week before Christmas one year, the two boys, now six and three, disappeared for the good part of an afternoon. They were in Drew's bedroom cooking up something while I was busy cooking up some of my own holiday recipes in the kitchen.

Trusting Drew to be careful with his brother was really pretty simple. Jerry and I included Drew in Matthew's care from the beginning, and, though Drew knew Matthew was fragile, he also knew Matthew would not break. If Matthew cried or needed his diaper changed while they played together, Drew invited me to help. Otherwise, he placed the *Do Not Enter* sign outside his bedroom door, which meant an artistic endeavor was in progress. I honored the sign's request.

Drew kept Matthew entertained by his constant chatter

while he prepared all the dialogue and costumes. It did not matter that Matthew was nonverbal; his infectious giggle kept Drew going. The more animated his brother became, the louder Matthew giggled. Laughter is the fuel that kept our entire family going.

Arriving home early that evening, Jerry finished setting the table while he filled me in on his workday. As a stay-at-home mom, I was eager to hear what went on in his adult world. We enjoyed our few minutes alone.

Shortly, though, I called to the boys, "Drew, dinner's ready. Do you need Dad to come get Matthew?"

Then we heard something. Jerry and I turned to each other with questioning frowns: *Do you hear what I hear?* Bells. We headed toward the bedroom door. More bells. The door flew open, and oh, what a sight was before our eyes.

Matthew's nose was painted bright red. *My lipstick?* I wondered. *When did Drew get it out of my room?* Reindeer antlers were fixed atop Matthew's head, and he wore his Christmas sweatshirt and pants. Drew had managed to change Matthew's entire outfit and get him onto his toy horse. Matthew held onto the handles that protruded from the toy horse's head, with his feet dragging on the ground, and giggled, fighting to keep his balance as Drew nudged the riding horse from behind. They slowly made their way into the living room.

Around Matthew's chest was a large, belt-like apparatus that had bells on it. How had Drew gotten the sleigh bells off the door without my seeing or hearing him? Intent on not being caught, he had obviously sneaked around the house, gathering his props quietly. Behind the reindeer, holding the reins, stood Santa Claus, complete with cotton-ball beard, stocking hat, red sweatshirt stuffed with a pillow, and cowboy boots.

"Ho, ho, ho!" Santa bellowed. "Rudolph and I came by to say, Merry Christmas!"

Santa shook the reins, causing the bells to ring, and Rudolph to giggle his head off. Jerry and I laughed so hard we cried. Drew burst into laughter as well. If there were any more lines in the play, he was too tickled to say them.

Fighting back the temptation to micromanage Drew with Matthew was difficult sometimes, but on that particular day things worked out just fine. The present Drew gave his Dad and me was better than any of the beautifully wrapped gifts under the tree.

Reining in Big Brother

Even the best eight-year-old in the world, however, can have a total lapse of judgment about what is good, safe, and appropriate.

"What were you two thinking!" I screamed at the top of my lungs at Drew and his best friend, TBird.

The kids and I had arrived at our friends' house for our regularly scheduled workday. We cleaned each other's houses, alternating weeks. This turned a not-so-pleasant task into fun for everyone because it allowed Drew and his buddy time to get together and play, and my friend and I could visit. The boys did not mind Matthew hanging out with them as long as he wasn't fussy or crying. He had started out a bit whiny that day, but the boys figured out a way to soothe him.

It was a beautiful day in early summer. The kids were out of school and happy to be outside. The days of soaring Texas temperatures, when the air conditioners ran nonstop, were a month away, so the early-morning breeze blowing through the house felt refreshing. Laughter from the three boys blew in with the breeze while we cleaned. Whatever they were doing sounded like fun.

Suddenly, something I could not identify flew by the den window, temporarily taking my eye off the job at hand. Waiting a minute to see if it would appear again, I returned to my dusting when it didn't.

A few minutes later, I saw something go by again, and this time I saw red, literally and figuratively.

"What in the world?" I said under my breath, frozen and unable to move, not wanting to believe what I suspected I had seen. Had that really been Matthew in his wheelchair I saw streaking by the window?

Matthew's wheelchair was a Swedish model: bright red, sporty, sturdy, all-terrain type. I guess it had a racecar-quality look to two eight-year-olds. It became apparent what the flashes were going by the window. Gathering my wits about me, I rushed outside.

Drew was at the bottom of the driveway, shouting, "Let 'im rip!"

Before I could yell, "Stop!" TBird released the wheelchair, and it careened down the hill. Matthew's arms and legs flailed; his laughter floated through the neighborhood.

My screeching voice, accompanied by the look of horror on my face, stopped the boys dead in their tracks.

"What in the world are you doing? Don't you know how dangerous this is? You could have killed Matthew."

Drew had caught his brother, swiftly turning the chair so it was between him and me. "But Mom," Drew shot back defensively, "Matthew loves it. I made sure his seatbelt and harness was on good. The hill isn't that big. He's not fussing anymore. It isn't dangerous. Didn't you hear him laughing?"

Yes, I had heard the laughter. And, it *was* the sweetest sound. All the things Drew had said were true. Well, almost all. It *was* dangerous. The chair could have tipped over.

Following a lengthy discussion about safety, the boys wisely chose their next activity, which involved water pistols. Matthew loved the water.

Two Kinds of Special

Drew grew up being told he was special, and that Matthew was also special.

Webster's Dictionary defines special as "surpassing the usual: exceptional." Another meaning is "distinct among others of a kind: singular." Webster described each child perfectly. They were each a different kind of special.

Another definition is: "esteemed: close," which describes the relationship between the boys. Drew wrote a paper in elementary school titled "Special." It began: "I have many reasons for being special. One of those reasons for being special is that I have a great family, especially my brother who is very different in a way." After talking about sports and his classes, Drew ended his paper with: "I may not look special outside, but on the inside, being special comes from the heart."

Drew wasn't the usual kind of brother. He was exceptional. I discovered what an exceptional young man Drew was becoming when I told him it was okay if he didn't like his brother. He was ten at the time.

Matthew had been very sick for several weeks. When we weren't in a doctor's office or hospital, we were homebound. Jerry was frustrated because it was an extremely busy time at work, and he was torn between his job and home. I was worn out from trying to be the glue that kept our family from falling apart during this stressful time.

We were all a mess, including Drew, who had been acting grumpy, which was out of character for him. I could not help Jerry or myself with our feelings, and I knew from past experiences that we would maneuver our way through this rough patch, but I thought I could help Drew, who had been receiving very little attention.

It was time to sit down and have one of our mother-son talks that could cause Drew's eyes to roll in directions I didn't think were possible. I had read somewhere that it is a good thing if, as a parent, you give your children permission to have bad and negative feelings. It is nothing to be ashamed of, and is perfectly normal.

I hesitantly began my speech with, "I realize things have been pretty tough around here, bud. Being frustrated and mad at your brother are normal feelings for you to have. It's okay if you don't like him right now."

Drew's eyes suddenly stopped rolling, and he looked straight at me. The stunned look came first, followed by his raised voice: "What did you just say?"

I continued sympathetically, "I know you love your brother dearly. So, it's okay if you don't like him right now." I smiled and thought, *This is good; I gave him permission, and he will confess.*

"What are you talking about, Mom? Of course I love Matthew. And, I like him too. I know he doesn't want to be sick. Don't you know he can't help it?" Drew got up from the table and walked away from me shaking his head, leaving me to process my thoughts.

Drew was *exceptional*. He was a mature thinker at a young age. Even if he had negative thoughts or feelings toward Matthew, he let his love for Matthew conquer them. Being special comes from the heart, just like he said in his essay.

California Dreamin'

Our most adventurous family vacation took place the summer after Matthew turned eight. It felt like Drew's entire fifth-grade class was packing to go on some exciting summer vacation, somewhere other than to a relative's home, and Jerry and I wanted to give Drew that same experience. We realized that, as Matthew got physically bigger, it would only be more difficult to tackle a trip like the one we dreamed of.

California was the destination we chose. With the Fodor's guidebook packed in our carry-on, we began our great adventure.

We landed in San Diego and picked up our roomy rental car, filling it to the brim with suitcases, diapers, a wheelchair, and backpacks. First stop: the San Diego Zoo. One of Drew's friends had moved to San Diego and was able to join us for the day. The boys had a ball. Matthew, worn out from the flight, was content to be pushed around the zoo in his wheelchair, and catnap throughout the day. Our vacation was off to a great start.

We spent several days leisurely making our way up the coast to San Francisco, stopping at several memorable attractions, including Hearst Castle, which was a highlight of the trip for all of us—not necessarily for its beauty or history but because of the way we were treated.

The castle sits impressively on a hill that overlooks the ocean. We made our way up to the departure area and waited patiently for the tour guide. Well, at least three of us waited patiently. Matthew became quite vocal, making sounds of displeasure. He preferred to be indoors, especially when it was windy. His whining whipped up like the ocean breeze, making the other tourists visibly uncomfortable.

"Let me take him to the car," I whispered to Jerry, knowing he enjoyed history much more than I do; he and Drew had really been looking forward to the tour. We were used to tag-teaming with Matthew, taking turns removing him from situations when it became apparent that would be best. A quiet ride in the car was all Matthew needed. We'd be fine.

I turned to make my way to the car and spotted an official-looking gentleman in a blue blazer heading toward our family. *He is probably coming to ask us to quiet Matthew down*, I thought. I prepared to make an even hastier exit with Matthew.

"Would your family like a private tour of the castle?" he said in an official tone.

What? Shocked, I heard him repeat the question.

"Would you like to come with me for a private tour? It would be my pleasure to be your guide."

Jerry, Drew, and I perked up, all nodded yes, and smiled at Matthew in his wheelchair. The man ushered us past the other guests, leading the way for our grateful family. Once inside, Matthew calmed down and rode around in silence. The tour was fascinating, and our knowledgeable leader treated us like royalty.

At the end of the tour we thanked him multiple times for his kindness. He was very humble and acted like he had done nothing out of the ordinary. Someone once beautifully said, "Sympathy sees and says, 'I'm sorry.' Compassion sees and says, 'I'll help.' When we learn the difference, we will make a difference." This compassionate man made a difference for us.

After the tour, as we drove north on the California coast, Drew started to hug and tickle Matthew in the backseat. Their giggles made Jerry and me smile.

"Wow! You did it, Matthew. You got us a private tour!" Drew continued, "Way to go, bro. You're the man. Never underestimate the power of the handicapped!"

The power of the handicapped? I thought. *How about the power of brotherly love?*

As the trip progressed, with Drew proudly pushing his brother's wheelchair, more doors opened to us because of Matthew's disability. Stares inevitably came, and we just smiled back, knowing some people viewed us with sympathy, others with compassion. The vacation was not an easy one, but it was worth the few times we encountered adversity. We were able to take a real family vacation, just like all our other friends and Drew's classmates, creating wonderful memories for our very special family.

Too Quick to Judge

Drew worked for a newspaper publisher, and scored free movie passes each week when he was sixteen. Matthew's love of movies made for the perfect brotherly outing. They were a pair: Drew, six feet tall, baggy jeans riding low on his skinny frame, shaved head; and Matthew, hands either flapping or in his mouth as he rode in the car and wheelchair, very cute but obviously mentally challenged.

When they arrived home from a movie one evening, Drew was noticeably upset.

"Was Matthew fussy in the movie theater, bud?" I asked.

"Nah. He was fine," Drew muttered as he buried his head in the refrigerator.

I could tell *something* had happened, so I kept prodding. After grabbing a Coke and making small talk, Drew finally opened up.

The theater they went to shared a parking lot with Dave and Buster's, a young adult, upscale hangout that offered food and games. Parking was at a premium.

"Thanks, Matt," Drew had said as he hung the handicapped tag from the rear view mirror and parked the car in the last handicapped space close to the door. He was grateful he did not have to go very far with Matthew in the cold.

Drew slid out of our small SUV and headed toward the back to unload Matthew's wheelchair. Halfway to the back of the car, he saw and heard an angry man approaching like a dive-bomber.

"Who do you think you are parking in a handicapped spot? Do you think you're better than everyone else? Are you too lazy to park out there like I did?" He pointed and shouted without taking a breath.

Drew stood there, looked at the ground, and did not say a word.

Catching up to her tyrannical husband, a meek woman said, "I am so sorry." To her husband, she said, "Please stop. Leave him alone. Let's just go inside."

The man ranted on, "My father is in a wheelchair, and I'm tired of people like you."

Opening the trunk, Drew pulled out Matthew's wheelchair and set it up. Without saying a word, he opened the passenger door, lifted Matthew out, placed him in the wheelchair, and buckled his seatbelt. As he unlocked the brakes on the wheelchair, Drew turned Matthew to face his accuser. He silently named him Jack-something.

"Jack's" wife was noticeably ashamed and embarrassed. Mr. Jack could not get his foot out of his mouth. Still silent, Drew pushed Matthew's chair around them and headed to the theater.

As the couple caught up, the woman said, "We're so sorry. We're so sorry."

"You have to understand," the man added. "You need to understand other people have taken advantage of handicapped parking spots, and with my father and all… I just thought you were like them. I…I…I'm sorry."

Unable to remain silent, Drew turned and yelled at the man: "I'm not like other people, and you are an idiot!"

Drew, unable to accept the apology, then said to the wife, "I feel sorry for you." The couple looked miserable.

Matthew sat in his chair, laughing and clapping, unable to comprehend the scene. He lightened Drew's mood, for the moment.

When Drew finished relating the story to me, I asked, "Why couldn't you forgive the man when he tried to apologize? It sounds like they felt really bad."

"Because, he was too quick to judge me, Mom. He stood there and yelled without giving me a chance to respond. He jumped to conclusions. Not all teenagers who pull into handicapped spots are doing it because they are lazy. Some have severely handicapped brothers, like I do, or handicapped parents, like he does. Maybe he'll remember that next time when he sees someone like me pull into a handicapped spot. I hope so."

"I hope so too, Drew."

"Anyway, the movie was great, and Matthew had a good time. That's what counts," Drew said, smiling on his way to his bedroom "Oh, and hey, Mom!" Drew shouted from the second floor, "The folks at the paper said I could get more tickets next week, so I'll take Matthew again."

They Don't Know My Brother

A few years later Drew moved away to college. The winter of his freshman year, the day after Matthew was diagnosed with a rare, deadly cancer, Jerry, Matthew, and I made the hour-and-a-half drive to deliver the news to Drew in person.

I had called him the night before and said, "We all miss you, so we're coming to take you to brunch tomorrow morning."

"But Mom," Drew said. "I just saw you guys last weekend. What's up?"

"Oh, nothing," I said with tears welling in my eyes. "How about meeting us at Cracker Barrel at ten o'clock?" I asked, trying to keep my voice cheerful.

"Whatever you say, Mom."

He had heard my voice crack. Why else would he have been so agreeable? Weekends at college usually meant you could stay in bed until noon. Normally, he would have argued.

The next morning we all met at the restaurant. Jerry and I decided to wait until after breakfast to tell Drew the news.

We could barely eat. Jerry and I sat there, making small talk, rearranging the food on our plates, pushing it from one side to the other with our forks.

"Okay, guys, where are you moving?" Drew blurted out, tired of the small talk.

"What?" Jerry and I said at the same time.

"I figured it out. You're moving. Why else would you guys come up to take me to breakfast?"

Jerry and I looked at each other, choking back the tears.

"Your brother is *really* sick, Drew," Jerry slowly said. "We need to talk."

"What do you mean?" Drew demanded. "He looks fine to me, besides his little cast on his arm where they took that cyst out. Okay, he looks a little tired too."

I squeezed Jerry's hand under the table and took over delivering the news the doctors had given us. I fought to keep my composure as I started to explain: "Your brother has cancer. That little cyst turned out to be a deadly form of soft tissue cancer. It is aggressive, and both doctors agree he probably has only a year to live."

The color went out of Drew's face. He looked at Matthew, who sat next to Drew laughing at something, then back to Jerry and me directly across the table from him. Jerry, Drew, and I sat there in silence staring through misty eyes at each other.

Drew was the first who was able to speak. "But they don't know Matthew. Doctors have said he was going to die before, and look, he's still here," he said as he put his arm around Matthew's shoulder and pulled him close.

Matthew smiled up at Drew, who had tears in his eyes. Drew said, "They don't know my brother. You can beat this, Matthew. I know you can. I just know you can. You'll be fine." Matthew kept smiling, not understanding a word, as Drew pleaded with him.

Jerry and I drove home with Matthew in silence. Drew went back to his dorm, convinced Matthew would once again beat the odds. We were not as optimistic as Drew was about Matthew's future.

Was another miracle out there for our blessed Mattie?

Five Years Later

Jerry and I were in the front row of the chapel looking back, along with all the other guests, at the entrance. Right on cue Matthew entered, accompanied by one of Drew's fraternity brothers. With his left arm raised in the air leading the way for balance, Matthew proceeded in his awkward gait toward the altar. Since he was unable to wear the typical dress shoes due to his leg braces, the tuxedo shop outfitted Matthew in black formal sneakers to accessorize his tux. It was quite a fashion statement.

Knowing we witnessed a miracle, Jerry and I had tears running down our cheeks. Watching from the altar as Matthew slowly made his way forward, Drew and Pastor Adam also realized they witnessed a miracle. Matthew, an excellent ring bearer and the most perfect brother Drew had ever hoped for, had made it to the wedding. It was his finest hour.

Part Three

No Regrets, Only Rewards

9

The Final Four: Fear, Funeral, Fulfillment, and Faith

*"So we fix our eyes not on what is seen,
but on what is unseen. For what is seen is
temporary, but what is unseen is eternal."*
- 2 Corinthians 4:18

In a Blink

Fewer than three months after Matthew's finest hour, he passed away. I had heard over the years about how people who are dying can "hold on" for something; a birthday, holiday, homecoming, reunion, and Mattie did just that.

The year before the wedding had been filled with numerous trips to doctors' offices. We dealt with high fevers, infections, bouts with the flu, decreases in appetite, fatigue, nausea, and never could pinpoint the culprit. His contagious laughter echoed through the house less frequently, replaced by moans and groans. One day Mattie would be his old self; the next day he would be uncomfortable, with strange symptoms. I kept praying he would make it to Drew's special day. He did. And, two days after the wedding, Matthew turned twenty-one. Another miracle.

Then he was done. Matthew started sleeping more and eating less. He was in constant pain or discomfort. From one doctor to the next, Matthew endured innumerable blood tests and X-rays while we desperately tried to figure out why he was so sick. The tests revealed that something was terribly wrong, but exactly what that something was eluded everyone.

Jerry and I noticed how his quality of life slowly deteriorated. Life had become too much of a struggle for him; he was fading. We needed to let go, which was more gut-wrenching than anything we had ever done. No more surgeries, no more hospitals, no more blood tests, no more X-rays.

Matthew deserved to have his days filled with the things he loved most: family, friends, Disney movies, Final Four games—both live and previously taped—music, rides in a convertible, and trips to Sonic for soothing, refreshing drinks.

Godsend

Hospice provides comfort and support to patients and their families when a life-limiting illness no longer responds to cure-oriented treatments. Jerry did not think we needed the help doctors told us Hospice could provide. After all, he said, we were surrounded by an incredible army of friends who were already walking with us, acting as our stretcher bearers, knowing they would be there for Matthew's final journey. We did not need strangers to come on board.

Jerry is now the first to admit that those *strangers* I adamantly insisted we invite into our lives are the ultimate angels here on earth. One of the first blessings we received from them was a small recliner. Lifting Mattie from his glider had become very painful for him. He was too low to the ground, and being pulled up by his arms caused him distress. The hospice team took note of this and ordered a chair to be brought to the house. This chair was higher, with a foot rest that came up, allowing him to sit up with his fluid-swollen legs and feet in an elevated position. The chair could magically catapult him up, out, into our arms, to a standing position, with the switch of a lever.

After tucking Mattie into bed each night, Jerry and I raced, each trying to beat the other to the magic chair in order to recline and relax. Whoever did not make it to the chair ended up on the comfortable, overstuffed couch next to it, which was covered with Matthew's cancer quilt.

Five years earlier, when Matthew was diagnosed with cancer, a dear friend of ours went to bed one evening feeling totally helpless, asking God how she could possibly help this young man she had grown to love. The message she received was emphatic: *You are not a quitter; you are a quilter.* The quilt she made Mattie was bold and beautiful; a Happy Quilt that made it impossible to look at him all wrapped up in it, and not smile. Although this friend was thousands of miles away, she figured out a way to wrap her loving arms around our family.

We found that Hospice cares not only for the patient but for the family as well. Each day a visiting nurse or doctor came by the house to check on how comfortable Matthew was, adjusted medications as needed, and asked how they could better minister to our family. I discovered that the people working with Hospice are much like the ministers we already knew, extending the loving care God wants us all to receive. They were God's hands and feet, just as our friends and family were.

After a nurse witnessed Matthew listening to one of his praise music CDs, and seeing the joy and comfort the songs brought him, a music therapist was unexpectedly added to the Hospice team. She showed up with her guitar and beautiful voice, and serenaded Mattie as he rested comfortably in his recliner. The team kept him as pain-free as possible, which allowed him to enjoy all his visitors and his family.

Little Room for Fear

He experienced simple joys and pleasures up to the end: sitting on the bench on the front porch, watching his daddy on the riding lawn mower; snuggling on the couch with his bubba, Drew; laughing a little as friends did all in their power to see his million-dollar smile one last time.

Matthew was surrounded by classmates, neighbors, pastors, family, and our friends. So many people filled our house with hope and love that, although we feared the end, that feeling did not consume us. We were grateful for each and every day we had with Mattie and each and every person in his life. Our focus remained on living each day to the fullest.

Jerry, Drew, and I were all with Matthew when he passed away. Drew was the first to speak. He looked at his brother then at Jerry and me, and said, "He looks so peaceful." No more pain. No more suffering. No more tears. Matthew, our gift from God, was going back to God.

I left Jerry and Drew with Mattie for a minute to let Pastor Adam know he had died. When he arrived at the house and entered the bedroom to pray over Matthew one last time, praise music played quietly in the background. He also noted how peaceful our precious man looked as he read Psalm 139 (NRSV):

> *O Lord, you have searched me and you know me. You know when I sit and when I rise; you perceive my thoughts from afar. You discern my going out and my lying down; you are familiar with all my ways. Before a word is on my tongue you know it completely, O Lord. You hem me in—behind and before; you have laid your hand upon me. Such knowledge is too wonderful for me, too lofty for me to attain. Where can I go from your Spirit? Where can I flee from your presence? If I go up to the heavens, you are there; if I make my bed in the depths, you are there; if I rise on the wings of the dawn, if I settle on the far side of the sea, even there your hand will guide me, your right hand will hold me fast. If I say, "Surely the darkness will hide me and the light become night around me," even the darkness will not be dark to you; the night will shine like the day, for darkness is as light to you. For you created my inmost*

*being; you knit me together in my mother's
womb. I praise you because I am fearfully
and wonderfully made; your works are
wonderful, I know that full well. My frame
was not hidden from you when I was made in
the secret place. When I was woven together
in the depths of the earth, your eyes saw my
unformed body. All the days ordained for me
were written in your book before one of them
came to be.*

Fearfully and wonderfully made. Indeed, Matthew was.

Preparations

We planned Mattie's funeral so many times over his
twenty-one years, you would think we'd have been totally
prepared. I prided myself each season on having all set which
outfit I would wear in case Matthew passed away. Not this
time. In many ways I had tried to ignore the fact that the end
was coming. It reminded me of the day he was born, and how
I did not even realize I was in labor. You unknowingly protect
yourself from the hurt you know is coming. *How in the world
can I go shopping now?* I wondered the day after he died.

There are people who have a sixth sense about who needs
what, and when. Preacher's Daughter was born with that
sense. She showed up at the hospital over the years at just the
right times, stopped by the house when I was ready to give
up, called out of the blue to say she had a treasure to drop off
for Matthew, and in the end, she said, "I will be glad to shop
for your dress for Mattie's funeral." PD, with her enviable
sense of style, not only took care of me but found the perfect
coordinating tie for Jerry as well. We were a mess inside but
sure looked good on the outside, thanks to PD.

Angel Chris took care of all the photo collages for the
funeral. Her sweet husband popped in to see Mattie the last

weeks of his life and leave with another box or envelop full of pictures to sort pictures and get ready for the funeral we knew was growing closer.

We chose the song "I Can Only Imagine," by MercyMe, to complement the video we planned. There were boxes and books full of pictures, taken from the day he was born to the day he passed away. We pictured Mattie in our minds singing the lyrics, which dream about what it will finally be like once we pass through this life. In our imaginations, Mattie's voice was accompanied by his praise leader hero on the piano. The chorus is particularly striking:

> *Surrounded by your glory,*
> *What will my heart feel?*
> *Will I dance for you, Jesus,*
> *Or, in awe of you, be still?*
> *Will I stand in your presence,*
> *Or to my knees will I fall?*
> *Will I sing hallelujah?*
> *Will I be able to speak at all?*
> *I can only imagine*
> *I can only imagine*

The Service

It was perfect in every way. Just like Mattie. Pastor Adam began the celebration of Matthew's life, saying he profoundly influenced the world around him.

Mentor Man read two letters at the service that I had written from Matthew's perspective. The first was to Jerry:

To my Earthly Father,

Before I was even given to you, I heard you shared with Mom after learning about my very rare genetic makeup: "He may be the cream of the crop." I'm not exactly sure if I was, but you always made me feel that way. You spruced me up with your acquired barber skills, and took me everywhere, proud I was your son.

When Mom would get overwhelmed with me, I remember you saying, "You can always put him out on the curb on Friday." Yikes! I knew you were only saying that to get her whipped back into shape, and it never failed. You were Mom's "other rock" when she could barely stand.

You showed Drew what it truly meant to be a man of God and what a husband and father really look like. He has a great start on being a good husband, and I know he will follow in your footsteps when it is his time to become a father.

Your faith is envied by many. You were the encourager, comforter, and provider who helped God keep my earthly family strong for my twenty-one incredible years. You brought Romans 8:28 alive for our family: "And we know that in all things God works for the good of those who love him, who have been called according to his purpose." Thank you, Dad, for everything.

The next letter was to Drew:

*Twenty-one years ago, when Mom told
you I wouldn't make it out alive, you knew
differently. Over the years, you would always
remind our folks, "They don't know my
brother" when we would all get news about
my medical challenges and opportunities.*

*Romans 5:3-4 reminded me of you and me:
"We also rejoice in our sufferings, because we
know that suffering produces perseverance,
perseverance character; and character, hope.
And hope does not disappoint us, because
God has poured out his love into our hearts
by the Holy Spirit, whom he has given us."*

*We both suffered, yet you always had hope,
an unbelievable character, and perseverance.
I remember you saying on countless
occasions, "Never underestimate the power
of the handicapped." If I could have spoken,
you would have heard me say, "Never
underestimate the power of my brother."*

*Thank you for giving me countless
opportunities over the years. I would not have
gone to half the places I did or experience
half the joys I did had it not been for you. The
greatest joy I had was being your ring bearer.
Thank you for that honor.*

*May God continue to bless you, Bubba, and
may you continue to have hope.*

While preparations were made for the funeral, Jerry caught wind that I had shared something special about his and Drew's roles in Mattie's life. He phoned Mentor Man with his thoughts so they could be included in the service as well:

> Ann was Matthew's chief medical officer, his physical therapist, his director of education, the spiritual liaison for the whole family, the CEO of whatever Matt needed. She was his special education advocate. Most importantly, she was Matthew's mom.

Drew had Mentor Man share the famous thoughts of Jim Valvano, an inspirational basketball coach who won an Espy Award, and someone Drew admired:

> To me, there are three things we all should do every day. We should do this every day of our lives. Number one is laugh. You should laugh every day. Number two is think. You should spend some time in thought. And number three is, you should have your emotions moved to tears—could be happiness or joy.
>
> But think about it. If you laugh, you think, and you cry, that's a full day. That's a heck of a day. If you do that seven days a week, you're going to have something special.

Drew and Matthew had that "something special" that Jim talks about. Mattie lifted his spirits whenever Drew was down with his incredible laughter; Matthew made Drew try harder, and he was certainly the best secret keeper a brother could have wished for.

While Pastor Adam shared his message, "Fearfully and Wonderfully Made," he was careful to point out that some people turn away from God, even blaming him, when a child like Matthew comes into their lives. Instead, he encouraged people to see Matthew and people like him as God does—of great beauty and worth. God used Matthew; Matthew was a means to accomplish God's purpose. The glory of God was revealed through Matthew in uncounted ways.

Jerry shared with Pastor Adam that he had planned a sermon in his own mind over the years for his son. His title was "Love Conquers All," meaning God's love. Matthew was used by God. And so was everyone who surrounded Matthew. He drove everyone to do what they thought was impossible, and brought out the best in all of us.

A portion from one of my favorite readings from *The Prophet*, by Kahlil Gibran, on joy and sorrow was shared during the service as well.

> *The deeper that sorrow carves into your*
> *being, the more joy you can contain. When*
> *you are joyous, look deep into your heart and*
> *you shall find it is only that which has given*
> *you sorrow that is giving you joy. When you*
> *are sorrowful look again in your heart, and*
> *you shall see that in truth you are weeping*
> *for that which has been your delight.*

Matthew brought immense joy and beauty into our lives. We are grateful and thankful to God to have had the opportunity to see the splendor of raising a handicapped child up close and personal.

Timing

Like so many times before, in the end, Matthew fell ill in the spring. Easter, with the promise of hope that the resurrection brings each of us, carried us through the darkest days of our lives. The sermon series Pastor Adam preached that spring was "The Bible and the Afterlife." The conclusion to the series was a sermon titled "What Is Heaven Like?" and was scheduled a year in advance. Adam preached it the weekend after Mattie passed away. His timing was perfect.

In that sermon, Pastor Adam asked the question about Matthew, "How could we not celebrate what he is now doing?" He described heaven as God's ultimate goal and ultimate destination for us all—paradise. Eternal life: This is what we were made for. Matthew has gone from this life to the next.

He left behind more than anyone could imagine, including the gift of actual sight for two gentlemen. I imagine they felt they received a miracle with their new corneas from our Miracle Man. Some people define a miracle as God breaking into, changing, or interrupting the ordinary course of things. God always did that with Matthew's life.

Carry On

After the funeral, we struggled to find a new normal; how to live life without Mattie. A friend thought a few days away was just what we needed. Jerry and I tried to act excited about the gift of a trip we were given to a five-star hotel on the east coast of Florida. It was the first time in twenty-one years we were going away without having to worry about whom we were going to get to take care of Matthew. Instead of being filled with eager anticipation, we were filled with an awful, empty feeling.

Our room overlooked a yacht club filled with the kinds of boats I had only ever seen in movies. After we unpacked, Jerry found me on the balcony, tears streaming down my face. "How do we do this?" I cried.

"We'll figure it out, Ann. We just need time," Jerry gently answered.

After we ate dinner, we strolled around the resort in silence. Spotting the pool, we decided that would be our first stop after breakfast the next morning. Back in our room, we climbed into the oversized, over-pillowed, overstuffed bed—total luxury, wasted on us. Jerry fooled with the TV clicker, switching from channel to channel. Suddenly, he stopped.

Larry King, suspenders and all, was on the TV screen. *We never watch him,* I thought. *This is pitiful. Surely there is something better on.*

Then Jerry and I heard a message God knew we needed to hear: "Don't let the sting of the loss erase the joy of the life."

Larry King was interviewing Art Linkletter, who had lost a son. That was Art's response to the question of how he dealt with his son's death.

Our time away was a gift. We were able to reflect on all we had been given through Matthew. It was good.

10 He Lives On

"Give, and it will be given to you." - Luke 6:38

The Gift of Life

Prior to Matthew's surgery for his scoliosis, I was told he would require at least four units of blood. *Where does it come from? Will there be enough of his type? Can we donate ahead of time?*

Finding answers for all of my questions before Mattie underwent any procedure gave me a sense of power. Knowledge is power when you enter uncharted territory; knowledge is the required roadmap. Not all healthcare professionals appreciated my relentless, unquenchable thirst for knowledge, although, the good news was, the majority did. Living near relatively large cities enabled us to have Matthew cared for at several outstanding teaching hospitals. Jerry and I found that our honesty and openness with these doctors, who wanted to learn, led them to be honest and open with us.

They informed me that the Community Blood Center supplied the blood for the hospitals in the Kansas City area, and I should contact them, that they would give me all the information I needed about how it would work.

As always, I shared my anxiety about the upcoming surgery with my friends. Jerry affectionately states with a laugh, "You never have to guess what is on Ann's mind. She will tell you even if you are not interested."

Many of my friends were connected to the relatively new, small church we had discovered in the elementary school in Kansas a few years earlier. Getting involved was simpler than I thought, and I found myself unexpectedly working as the church receptionist as well as Pastor Adam's secretary shortly after we joined. With its first building project underway, I was blessed to be part of an energetic and visionary staff.

"Matthew needs blood for his upcoming surgery," I blurted out just as the caller's business was finished. This church family was so tight that, three or four calls later, I hardly had a chance to say, "Good Morning," before the person calling in said, "I heard Mattie needs blood for his surgery. I can donate."

This happened five or six times in one day. I felt relieved. There would be enough blood. My next step was to get in touch with the folks at Community Blood Center, like I had been told, to find out more details.

What I learned threw me in another direction. It did not seem right that blood donated specifically for Matthew would be discarded if not used. After all, I had heard repeatedly that it was the gift of life. *How could any extra be discarded? Why would they do that? What about other folks who needed blood? What if they were able to benefit?* The guidelines for donating for one specific person are very cut and dried.

Whenever an opportunity or problem was arose, either in the church or our family, my young pastor and new boss had a persuasive way of encouraging me to be part of the solution. After researching, praying, and talking with Jerry, I sat down and wrote a letter.

Dear Pastor Adam,

In following God's calling, turning every negative in our lives into something positive, Jerry and I would like to propose establishing a semi-annual blood drive at Church of the Resurrection.

We have been told Matthew needs at least four units of blood for his upcoming surgery.

*Two options we were given in securing the
needed blood are: Ask friends with the same
blood type to donate, or, use community
blood.*

*Fortunately, after discussing Matthew's
surgery with several friends, we believe we
have more than enough volunteers willing to
donate blood. However, instead of limiting
ourselves to only Matthew's needs, it is our
thought that the United Methodist Church of
the Resurrection is at the point in its growth
where we should begin sponsoring a semi-
annual blood drive for our church family
and community. We would like Matthew's
upcoming need to serve as the springboard for
our church-sponsored blood drive.*

Pastor Adam endorsed our proposal, throwing his
full support behind our efforts. It was amazing to see the
outpouring of folks who wanted to help Matthew in this way.
Almost fifty folks came to the first blood drive we had at
church, resulting in forty-two units of blood. It helped stock
the shelves at the Community Blood Center, to ensure that
anyone—not just our Mattie—would have the gift of life—
blood—when needed.

Saving Lives

The Blood Drive Ministry has grown to an astonishing
level. We sponsored two drives in 1995 then bumped it to
three per year until 2005, and have hosted quarterly drives
ever since. In 2010, Jerry and I had the honor of accepting the
Association of Donor Recruitment Professionals Organization
Award in Seattle on behalf of the church.

With the amount of blood Church of the Resurrection

has collected, they recognized the role we play in sustaining the community's blood supply. We accepted the award, accompanied by the praise given:

> *Church of the Resurrection has a group of volunteers who help with every drive. Donors are given the VIP treatment from the moment they walk in until the time they leave. They feel appreciated, and that's one of the reasons many donors come to all the drives, and bring new people. They know it will be a great experience.*

Bone marrow drives have been held in conjunction with several of the blood drives, resulting in hundreds of people registered in the Be the Match Marrow Registry. Several bone marrow matches have come from within our church and community as a result of these drives.

Matthew came to the blood drives. After he and I walked around the donor tables, thanking each person for their donation, he sat in his wheelchair watching Disney movies in a space created to keep our donors' children entertained. At first, some of the children, especially the smaller ones, were frightened by Mattie. However, they grew accustomed to him over time, and flocked to his space when their parents came to donate. Occasionally I caught a glimpse of a little kid trying to share a cookie with Mattie. The interaction was worth the mess I had to clean up. His Disney movies still appear at each drive, and I always feel his presence there.

This life-saving mission has resulted in almost thirty thousand units of blood collected at Church of the Resurrection. One unit of blood can potentially save two lives. Almost sixty thousand lives have possibly been affected in such a profound way. Nationally, Church of the Resurrection is viewed as a top-ten blood-producing organization for our consistent high production over the past decade.

In 2012, a church member's life was saved as a result of discovering that her hemoglobin count was incredibly high at one of our blood drives. Carolyne shared her story:

Before giving blood, my finger was pricked to see if I was a candidate for giving. To my surprise, I was rejected due to an elevated hemoglobin count. I immediately called my doctor.

Over the next few weeks, I found myself going through a series of tests, and was sent to a hematologist for more extensive blood work-up. My hemoglobin and hematocrit counts were dangerously high, and I carried the JAK2 mutation. I was diagnosed with polycythemia vera, a rare blood disease that causes the body to make too many red blood cells, and if untreated could lead to death by heart attack or stroke. I was at that critical point. I then started the process of phlebotomies every two weeks for several months until my counts were in normal range.

I will never be able to give blood, and I will receive phlebotomies for the rest of my life. In my attempt to give the gift of life-saving blood, my own life was saved.

It is more blessed to give than receive. It works both ways; when you give you receive; in my case, it was the gift of life.

*With great gratitude, I thank the Joyner
family, who started the blood drive at the
Church of the Resurrection in honor of their
son Matthew. Thank you for saving my life.*

This letter, as well as others, reinforces Jerry's and my understanding that Mattie's life was worth more than any doctor ever imagined. His life touched and saved thousands of others and continues to do so.

Dreams Fulfilled

If you build it, they will come. That famous line from the movie *Field of Dreams* pertains to so many more things than the baseball field attracting players and fans that it refers to in the movie. Matthew's Ministry began at Church of the Resurrection as a result of people who answered a call, had a vision, and followed God's calling.

A few lines from "Abraham's Song," written by Lance Winkler, beautifully describe how I feel the congregation responded to Matthew.

> *Lord, I have heard your voice*
> *Saying I must go*
> *To a place I've never been before*
> *But if you walk with me*
> *If you take my hand*
> *Anywhere you are, Lord, is the promised land*
> *So I will set my eyes on Jesus,*
> *embracing the unknown*
> *I will sacrifice what's precious,*
> *though it's all I own*
> *I am just a pilgrim stranger on this sod*
> *I am looking for a city that's foundation is*
> *of God*

Shortly after our family joined the church, I began working alongside fellow staff members and volunteers to create Angel Care teams for each person who came to the church in need of the one-on-one assistance we offered through Matthew's Ministry. One of Mattie's best friends, Happy Guy, was among the original ten participants.

Prior to coming to Resurrection, his mother, Ultimate Patience, left him home each Sunday while she and her husband took turns going to worship alone. It was only after she heard me go on and on and on about how involved Jerry and I had become in our church family that she finally asked, "What do you do with Matthew?"

"He comes with us," I said simply, forgetting how unique our situation at the church was. "A volunteer meets us at the door, and he is taken to join his peers in Sunday school while Jerry, Drew, and I worship. Then another volunteer takes over while Jerry teaches Sunday school and Drew goes to youth group. They hang out with him and explore the outdoors, visit with folks in the hall, play with toys in the library, or snuggle on a bench."

As I talked, Ultimate Patience began shaking her head and sadly replied, "Well, you know Mattie is pretty docile compared to Happy Guy. I'm not sure anyone can handle him."

"Listen," I insisted, "our church family has a *whatever-it-takes* attitude, instilled by Pastor Adam. We will do whatever it takes to care for your whole family."

They joined shortly thereafter. Happy Guy communicates with his eyes, just like Matthew. To see them light up each time he enters church reminds his volunteers what Jesus said in Matthew 25:40 (NRSV): "Truly, truly I say to you, just as you did it to the least of these, who are my family, you did it to me."

Jerry and I have witnessed broken families becoming

whole again. One father of twin boys, who are part of Matthew's Ministry, wrote the following, which was shared at our Christmas gathering one year:

> I apologize for not being able to say thank you in person. However, we got out of routine today, and those of you with autistic children know that can be quite an adventure.
>
> We had stopped going to church altogether because we felt like we did not fit in. After a couple of years of longing to be part of a church community again, we decided to look for a place that could first and foremost meet the needs of our children. That is when we came across Church of the Resurrection and Matthew's Ministry.
>
> You have given my family the greatest Christmas gift we could have received this year. And that is the opportunity to again be part of a church family.

Each new program offered in the ministry has been an answer to prayers and desires that have been expressed by parents of children with special needs. Additional opportunities have resulted from the dreams of a team of committed volunteers and staff.

As I sat in a Matthew's Ministry committee meeting one day, the idea of a respite night came up. I must have looked really tired and worse for the wear from my three-year detour to Colorado, from which we had recently returned, because they all looked at me for a reaction. I just smiled and helped plan the evening.

When Jerry and I dropped Mattie off at the church to the first Family Night Out so we could go on a three-hour date, everyone who greeted us looked rested and up for the challenge.

Upon our return, it was plain to see that Jerry and I were now the rested ones, recharged to provide the ongoing care Mattie needed. The volunteers looked like Silly Putty that had been thrown against the wall. Their clothes were a bit disheveled, their hair was a mess, but tired as they were, they thanked us and the other parents for allowing them to watch our children. Jerry and I rushed home to put the next date on the calendar.

Blondie began volunteering around the same time the church began offering Family Night Out. When she originally signed up to be one of Matthew's Angel Care workers on Sunday mornings so Jerry and I could worship together, he successfully wrapped her around his little finger, melting her with his beautiful brown eyes and long eyelashes.

Run mostly by a handful of committed volunteers and parents of participants during the first ten years, the ministry had grown to a point that we needed to place someone in a staff leadership role. Blondie was Matthew's first choice. She shares:

> *When the opportunity to head up Matthew's Ministry was presented to me, I knew this was what I was meant to do, after searching for twenty-five years. Matthew lit the fire in me—possibly when I was running up and down the hallways of the church with him in his wheelchair at breakneck speed—and he rewarded me with deep belly laughs. I am certain God spoke through Matthew to encourage me to answer the call to dream big and to expand a special needs ministry.*

Faces in the Son

The ministry has grown exponentially from the small seeds of the one-on-one Sunday morning care and Family Night Out offerings that formed the foundation of Matthew's Ministry. Additional programs include youth and adult Bible studies where the participants can grow in their faith. There are also Sonflower Bakery, Ringers, and the Backpack Program. These are all opportunities for our participants to use their unique gifts to serve our church. The Sonflower Adult Learning Program, a daily program during the week, is a Christ-centered program with learning and enrichment activities for participants over twenty-one.

Each of these programs resulted from people, following Blondie's example, dreaming big. We adopted *Sonflower* in naming the programs because the sunflower, Kansas's state flower, always follows and reaches toward the light of the sun. In Matthew's Ministry, all participants follow the Son.

Volunteer Connie, who met Mattie the first day we visited Church of the Resurrection when it met in the gym, wrote "No Disabled Souls," which she has given me permission to print:

> *The good Lord works in mysterious ways,*
> *sure enough. And paradoxical ways too.*
> *Things aren't always what they seem to*
> *be, messed-up plans somehow work out*
> *better than the way we planned them, and*
> *grace defies logic. So it is with Matthew*
> *and everything—everyone—around him.*
> *How can this woman, this burdened mother,*
> *smile so? I remember thinking that surely*
> *this happy gal was not the mother of that*
> *little Matthew. And how can this family be*
> *so generous? Why would these people bother*
> *listening to anybody else's trivial, petty,*

ordinary problems? Why did this ambitious
young church decide to do what others would
not do? Didn't we have enough to worry
about, with babies in the corner and kids in
the storage room and never enough folding
metal chairs? What seemed like a burden
is revealed as a blessing. The spirit that has
been squashed, smashed, nearly stamped out,
soars—taking others with it. And if we quiet
ourselves, listening carefully, we learn that
the challenge is sometimes a calling. Paradox.

The Other Side

Jerry, Drew, and I continue to receive blessings from Matthew's Ministry as we volunteer our time in its various programs. "DJ Drew" enjoys near-celebrity status serving as the disc jockey at proms and dances, connecting with the guests in a magical way. On the dance floor at a recent event, a new volunteer approached me and asked, "Ann, if Matthew were still alive, what would he be doing now?"

Moved by her question, I smiled and said, "We would have him out of his wheelchair, holding onto him, swaying back and forth. He loved the music and loved to move."

Though she never got to meet Matthew, her desire to know more about him, as well as other participants, convinced me this was someone we needed to hold on to.

When the church offers Family Night Out, it is not only for the person with special needs but for their siblings as well. Each child deals with his or her unique family situation differently, as Drew witnessed one evening while sharing his story with them about what it was like to grow up with a brother like Matthew. The leader of the class told me he was exactly what the kids needed—someone who was captivating and real, and who spoke to them on their level. There was an instant connection.

The kids' questions tugged at Drew's heart. Statements like, "I have no friends because of my brother with Down syndrome" were hurled at him.

Drew tossed back, "How many of you know who Albert Pujols is?"

Several hands shot up. The kids smiled, probably thinking, *Okay, now we can talk about something fun—baseball.*

"Albert Pujols has a daughter with Down syndrome." Drew watched his audience carefully as he told them about this famous baseball player's family as well as other famous people who had kids with special needs.

Albert says, "The Pujols Family Foundation is a national, not-for-profit agency that exists to honor God and strengthen families through our works, deeds and examples. Since beginning this foundation in 2005, we have sought to help those living with Down syndrome here at home and to improve the lives of the impoverished in the Dominican Republic. Along the way, God has blessed us richly, and for those of you who have been a part of that journey, we offer our gratitude."

Drew went on to mention TV celebrities who have sons, daughters, brothers, or sisters with special needs. These were people these kids knew of, people who were happy and successful.

"Well, do you have any friends, Drew?" one young girl innocently asked.

"As a matter of fact, I do," Drew replied with a smile. "One of my best friends, who knew Matthew quite well, and his wife are actually here tonight. They got a babysitter for their two kids so they could come tonight and hang out with kids like your brother." Drew watched as a look of disbelief washed over her face. He knew exactly what she was thinking: *So people actually want to be with him?*

Like Drew's friends, I want to be with this little girl's brother, and all the other folks with special needs. Now, I am the one with disheveled hair looking like Silly Putty thrown against the wall by the end of a Family Night Out. It can be utterly exhausting. It can also be exhilarating.

I know better than anyone what my short three hours of hanging out with their kids means to their parents. There is no other place I would rather be when our church offers these nights once a month. The small gift I am able to give does not compare to the gift I receive.

Jerry and I also serve on Angel Care teams in Matthew's Ministry. We know the peace of mind parents feel as they walk into worship knowing their children are loved and valued by us and their church family. If that gift had not been given to us, neither Jerry, Drew, nor I would be who we are today. For this, we give thanks to God and to the churches that opened their doors to us. Galatians 6:10 says, "Therefore, as we have opportunity, let us do good to all people."

Amazing Grace, the class Matthew inspired at our first church in Arlington, Texas, has grown and evolved into a ministry that now involves additional classes, First Friday Respite Night for parents and caregivers, one-on-one buddies accompanying people who need extra assistance in regular classrooms, and a Vacation Bible School for people with special needs. As more and more children are diagnosed with unique problems, the church continues to be there to meet the needs of parents and the community.

Ring to the Glory of God

When Matthew passed away, we set up the Matthew Joyner Memorial Fund, knowing he had touched many people's lives who would want to remember him in a special way. We researched statues, looked at creating a garden on the church property; we even talked about placing a fish tank in the reception area of the church. They were nice thoughts but did not represent who Matthew was. Though I felt pressured to let people know how their gifts were used, Jerry and I were unable to agree on a course of action for quite some time.

When the Matthew's Ministry team met at my house more than a year later, I revisited my dream of having a special needs bell choir. Always the practical and down-to-earth leader of the group, Blondie said, "Ann, there is no one to lead it. There is no money left in the budget to buy the expensive equipment. This will not happen this year."

The newest member of our team, the mother of a Matthew's Ministry participant, spoke up confidently. "I played bells for years in Texas and have always wanted my daughter to play. I could be the director."

Another member spoke up, inquiring, "Where will we find the funds for the equipment?"

"Matthew's Memorial Fund!" I excitedly screamed. God's timing. Not mine.

We placed the initial order, requesting each bell handle to be inscribed with: *Ring to the Glory of God, In Matthew Joyner's Memory.*

Sonflower Ringers rapidly grew from one bell choir to two bell-and-chime choirs. Orders continue to be placed not only for bells and chimes but for performance vests. The groups' professional sound and look are a credit to a dedicated director and team of volunteers. Their performances leave audiences inspired, amazed by the talent these choirs possess and enthusiastically share.

A parent of a ringer acknowledged, "Each time I listen to my daughter play in a handbell choir concert, I think of my musical mother, who resides in Canada. Were it not for the Matthew's Ministry handbell choir, likely I would never have had the opportunity to see how my mom's love of music has been passed down to her special granddaughter. What a precious gift this is."

A niece says of her aunt, "I found it is never too late to start something new. My aunt was seventy-three years old when she started with the bell ringers, and in the time that she has been with them, I have seen her become more participative with less prompting. It makes them smile, and fills my heart with joy."

One participant shared, "I really like doing bells because it makes people happy to hear me play. When they clap really hard after each song, it makes me feel like I'm Hannah Montana!"

Matthew's lifelong love of music continues to be spread by his peers as they ring their way into nursing homes, worship services, and church conferences in Kansas and Missouri. Smiling, I dream of a Sonflower Ringers' bus taking them to their destinations in the future.

Coast to Coast and Beyond

In 2010, Blondie and I were invited to present a workshop at Accessibility Summit, a national conference for the disability community in Washington, DC. We were blessed to share the meaningful ministry that is being offered at the United Methodist Church of the Resurrection to members with special needs. Seeds were planted in the hearts of the audience, and spread across the country to grow similar programs.

Taking what you have learned, and sharing it with people outside your family or own small community, is central to Church of the Resurrection's teachings. Each year the church offers Leadership Institute, inviting church leaders from around the world and country.

After meeting a group at our Leadership Institute from Los Altos United Methodist Church in California, I was invited to speak to their congregation on Mother's Day in 2012.

Their church was ready to launch a special needs ministry, and they ask me to share how the church and my faith made a difference in my life as the parent of a special needs child. What I shared with them is the same message I took to the Ukraine, on mission trips our church sponsored in

2005 and 2008.

Three days after our first Christmas without Matthew, Jerry and I were on our way to visit the Methodist church in Chernivtsi, Ukraine. We struggled our first year without Mattie, and knew the mission opportunity presented to us in the fall was what God had prepared us for. Scared before takeoff, we jokingly said to each other, "If it weren't for Mattie, we would be headed to lie on some beach in Mexico."

Our mission team went to visit children with special needs and their families in their homes. While visiting with the passionate mom who dreamed of starting a ministry of assistance for families like hers in her community, I was asked by an interpreter how I did it. "How did you lead a life of joy while raising a handicapped child?" The interpreter repeated his question in Russian.

Tomara and I looked down at her beautiful, smiling son, his handicapped body so twisted and contorted. Then I gazed into her eyes, pointed skyward, and said, "Without God in my life, it would have been impossible."

AFTERWORD

A life that's not worth saving.

Those words are stuck in my mind. They haunt me now, in that they represent the attitude of many who share this title of humankind. It causes me to think that some consider life as nothing more than a business venture. If a profit is not to be made, if contributions are not apparent, then costs and risk are to be minimized as much as possible.

A young mother was told her unborn baby had a rare genetic deformity and that the baby would most likely be stillborn. The mother and father, grasping at hope that they could help their son, asked if the doctor could take the baby from the womb early, so as to allow for any surgery or treatment that would help the child survive. Those were the words that met this young, anxious, desperate couple. "It's a life that's not worth saving."

The child was born anyway, and he was born alive. He had many problems. He would be mentally retarded. He would be physically disabled. He would require constant medical attention.

"The baby will probably not live very long. Preparations should be made."

The child grew, as did the hearts, the trials, the faith, and the love of his parents and his older brother. All along the way, there were those who prayed, those who helped. There were also those who had no faith and those who just turned away.

"The child will not live to be 10...11...13..."

The boy continued to fight for life. With his parents and his brother, he would experience life. He would ride a wagon down a hill with his brother's help. He would take steps with a walker. He would learn to use a spoon. He would swim with the help of floats. He would ride a horse, drive a boat, move to music, and watch basketball.

There's more. He would see his family grow in faith and service, in ways they never dreamed of. His mother and father and brother would do things they never thought they were capable of doing.

There's even more. This boy endured many medical procedures, one where he needed blood. A request was made for the boy. Donors were found in his church family. In fact, that request grew into a regular blood drive that has yielded thousands and thousands of units of blood. This boy, whose parents were looking for a church family that could accommodate a handicapped child, was the catalyst of a new ministry that now administers to the needs of hundreds of children, youth, younger and older adults, and their families in a Christian environment where all are welcome.

I have seen it myself. In a place where people used to avoid contact with the handicapped, people now seek out and embrace these children of God.

This young man, Matthew Joyner, left us on April 20, 2005, to be with the Lord. He now dances with Jesus, speaking his first words in a song of joy. His struggles are over; he is free. The life that was not worth saving has touched the lives of literally thousands in profound ways. Now, what will we do with what he has taught us? What will we do with the inspiration he put in our hearts?

"I tell you the truth, whatever you did for one of the least of these brothers of mine, you did for me" (Matthew 25:40).

John R. Ross, friend and mission partner
Overland Park, KS

To read more on the ministry that was started from love for Matthew, go to *www.cor.org*, and click on Special Needs: Matthew's Ministry.